The Definitive Twitter Guide:

Making Tweets Work for Your Business

30 Twitter Success Stories From Real Businesses and Non-Profits

By Shannon Evans

To Caden
Thanks for all you do!

Cover Design by Matt Mikulsky, Chatter Creative
http://www.twitter.com/mikulsky

Developmental Editor - Shelley Schwinn Brownlow

Copy Editor – Jennifer A. Evans

Publishing Consultant Richard Geasey

www.bainbridgebusinesspress.com

ISBN: 1453703276

Library of Congress Control Number

Content is used with permission from author Denise Barnes.

Receive more mobile tips, tricks, and resources at:

Website: www.ikeepitfunky.com

Blog: http://blog.ikeepitfunky.com

Facebook: www.facebook.com/iKeepItFunky

Twitter: http://Twitter.com/iKeepItFunky

"iKeep It Funky" develops user-friendly tools tailored for people who want to take the convenience of the office on the go. "iKeep It Funky" also translates geek speak into everyday language, and removes the fear of using mobile technology. "iKeep It Funky" utilizes sound bytes to produce targeted nuggets of information.

This book is dedicated to:

Miss Hairston (pronounced "Haaston") who wadded up all my writing assignment in the first week of 7th grade. She gave me the impetus to learn how to type.

Miss Burgin, my 11th grade English and Latin teacher, who commended me on my Latin translations. She then chided me on my abundance of bullet points to discuss the impact of the Punic Wars. She gave me a passion for following brevity with pithy detail.

Mr. Jere Hoar, faculty member at Ole Miss who encouraged me to "never write anything more than a grocery list." He ingrained in me that ageless fear of the editor's dreaded red pen and made me work ten times harder to find my own voice and my own unique style.

Richard B. Evans who claimed I would never get published because I had "too much to say and not enough paper to say it; nor, an audience that wanted to hear it." His words were the challenge that motivated me to seek the right audience and to hopefully craft my ideas into words that people want to hear.

Pat Ross who always said, "If you think you can't, you won't. If you think you can, you will." Momma, I KNOW I can and I did.

Shelley Brownlow, founding member of the Pink Mojito Lacrosse Society and Harbor Office editor extraordinaire, your ever handy red pen and pithy insights as always are dead-on. Your wit and wisdom reigns supreme!

Jennifer A. Evans, some debts are never fully paid. You keep me on my toes both with your editing skills and your continuous push to expand the limits of my poor aching brain both on paper and beyond. With you on my team I can't go wrong.

Richard S. Eidens, my stalwart support system, I could never make any of this happen without your continued patience, kindness, and awesome singing talents. You are truly a one of a kind, special edition, once-in-a-lifetime best friend.

"A lot of people have been quoting me ever since I came to play for the Yankees in 1946. But, as I once said, I really didn't say everything I said. So now it's my turn. I want to give some of my famous advice to the graduates. First, never give up, because it ain't over 'til it's over. Second, during the years ahead, when you come to the fork in the road, take it. Third, don't always follow the crowd, because nobody goes there anymore. It's too crowded. Fourth, stay alert. You can observe a lot by watching. Fifth, and last, remember that whatever you do in life, 90 percent of it is half mental."

Excerpts from Yogi Berra's commencement speech as delivered to the Class of 1996, Montclair State University.

Table of Contents

Prologue: The Microblogging Revolution

What is microblogging and why does it matter? Social media is not some ethereal world that requires a PhD to navigate and apply to business. Social media marketing is nothing more than humans interacting and communicating about goods, services, tools, opinions, and events. Blogs and microblogs are becoming more socially interactive as social media elements are integrated into the various delivery platforms. Bloggers are adding more video, audio, and even expanded SMS type capability to engage readers. Microblogging is similar to blogging in that people are posting updates about topics of interest to their followers, responding, and interacting; however, it differs in that it is much smaller in both content length and file size.

- What is social media marketing?
- What is Twitter?
- Why should I care what it is?
- Does it really matter to my business?
- Isn't this stuff for kids and techies?

Microblogging platforms like Twitter, Pownce, Jaiku, Hellotxt, etc are evolving into a social community where people connect, share, publish and collaborate to talk about companies and brands. They make recommendations, leave reviews, and seek advice. They complain and they complement, but mostly they create brand recognition within a community.

In the business world of the web, there is a social revolution occurring where the emphasis is on two-way communication. Businesses are encouraging their customers to engage directly with them on the web in forums, on blogs, and in social networks like Twitter and Facebook. Businesses and consumers are both depending on social media to share their customer service stories and to provide additional information that assists with buying decisions. This sharing of information and influence is helping traditional marketing methods to meet a timely demise.

According to Seth Godin in his book, *Permission Marketing*, traditional interruption based marketing/advertising model is dead. People have either become numb to it or have ceased to purchase from the push, push, push of marketers. Now consumers are hungry for ways to interact with companies and their products and even other consumers.

These savvy new consumers are using media tools like blogs, podcasts, social networks, and other social media to interact and connect. They want the freedom to connect, participate, and interact online about the goods they buy and the experiences they have on a daily and sometimes hourly basis.

Social Media Defined

Social media is difficult to define, but it is fairly unique and easy to separate from traditional media. Traditional media uses push marketing techniques that when used in the social media setting, it is regarded as spam. Try those techniques in a social media setting and see how ineffective they are. Your friends/followers will abandon you, block you, and publicly admonish you for your blatant sales behaviors.

Social media is about empowerment at the individual level. Participants can read or not read, follow or "unfollow", join or leave. It is all about individual choice. Social media is the way people naturally share ideas, content, thoughts, and relationships online. It is a place where people can create, comment, and add content within existing social sites. This is something that can't be done in mainstream media. When was the last time you could leave a comment after an article in the local print version of the paper?

The Internet has transformed our ability to share information. Savvy businesses are adapting to the rapidly shifting and changing Internet environment through blogging, podcasting, wikis, tweeting, and using various social networking media (YouTube, Facebook, Twitter, LinkedIn, etc) to broadcast information quickly. On average:

- There are 13 hours of video uploaded on the Internet per minute
- There are 13 million articles on Wikipedia.org
- Over 55% of the people on earth have a photo up on Flickr
- If Facebook was a country it would be the 8th largest country in the world based on population
- Twitter experienced a 1400% growth in one month period in 2009.

Source: http://thefuturebuzz.com/2009/01/12/social-media-web-20-Internet-numbers-stats/

Social media has created a unique and vibrant culture that allows for the exchange of ideas and information while allowing the sharing of thoughts and expertise. It also promotes people to offer their expertise to a broad audience of like-minded people, who belong to a community of listeners.

Due to the informal aspect of social media, honesty, humility, and earnestness are promoted and hucksters and self-promoting narcissistic members are shut down or quickly shunned by the group. The community itself creates the standards for conduct. Social media tends to be "self-policing". When members stray too far from the accepted behavior, they tend to be ostracized by the group.

While it is true that not everyone wants to use these social communities the same way; there are many different ways for participants to interact and stay within the accepted standards for behavior. Social media communities all boil down to finding the right community; a place where similar groups of people with similar goals and expectations connect online. It is important that as a participant, you find the right community that matches your style of connecting/sharing, and for whom your message appeals.

Social media is designed to be community oriented. And just like "real" communities, virtual communities rely on people who take part and contribute. Without "givers" community cannot exist! Building community is essential to the success of the group. Newcomers to social media often have the perception that one size fits all; many of them drop out after a short time, due to their inability to be proactive and work to effectively join and become a member of the community.

Social media is evolving and as such is a moving target. The technology and the social communities change rapidly. Some of it is fad driven, but this is for certain, social media is not one size fits all and it is here to stay.

Introduction: Social Media - Why We Should Care

90% of Americans are on the Internet. In the U.S., 3 out of every 4 people are participating in some form of social media. That's over 300 million people! World-wide 2 out of 3 people are participating in social media. That is over 5 billion people! You can't afford for your business to not be "found" on social media.

Social media tools help businesses share information and connect with potential customers. What business can succeed without getting to know its customers? What business can survive without being seen as a reliable place for information or products? Social media promotes and supports businesses prospecting for new customers, connecting with existing customers and listening to what is going on in their community and their industry. Social media is a powerful way to connect with people and other businesses. Connections ultimately keep you in business.

Social media is rapidly changing how a business shares information with their customers. Businesses today openly seek feedback, criticisms, reviews, and suggestions for future product and services development. Proactive progressive businesses are using social media to cultivate and manage their brand's reputation. They recognize the strength of social media's contribution to business in today's global economy.

Businesses that do not see their customers as participants in their community will struggle to understand all the hype of social media and will wither on the vine if they do not move to at least consider the possibilities that it presents.

Businesses that are willing to change and grow with the possibilities of social media will be the most successful in these uncertain economic times. Those who fear change or fail to explore any of the possibilities of social media will stagnate and possibly fold, once their customer base recognizes their stagnation.

> ***Tip:*** Successful brands follow this basic formula when monitoring social media:
>
> - Pay attention to what people are saying about you, your brand and your competition.
> - Decide what your company stands for and then draft a plan around it
> - No one really cares about your company name or your brand/logo, they care about what you or your brand does for them!
> - Creativity counts, as does building trust.

The Challenges of Social Marketing for Business

Social marketing meets with much skepticism and resistance in many of the more traditional corporate camps. Social marketing is not seen as complementary to their more traditional marketing channels. The perception is that the results are not achieved nearly as quickly with social media, as it is with more direct push marketing techniques like print advertising. Many marketing models create unrealistic timeline expectations for social media marketing metrics; when those unrealistic expectations are not met, any further attempts of using social media are abandoned.

A hurdle for many small businesses venturing down the social marketing path is the perception that the learning curve for each platform is too steep and too time consuming. There are limited resources to guide small business owners in acquiring the necessary skills quickly, so they do not waste valuable time.

Marketers think in terms of generating leads, gathering referrals, and creating a huge base of contacts. Without that huge collection of names and phone numbers stored in a huge rolodex, traditional marketers feel lost and not in control.

Finding a social media that successfully markets a company or organization requires that the end user first, finds tools that are comfortable to them and that they can relate to. They must then see the potential for use with their target market. When they find particular tools that do mostly what they want them to do, they begin to envision the potential of social marketing. They start thinking "what if."

The explosion of various forms of social media makes it difficult to decide which form and which format is worthwhile for professional organizations, businesses, business networks, and individuals. Social media can be used to connect groups of like-minded organizations and businesses to generate creative thought, collaborative work groups, or to inform and educate a company's customer base.

As a marketing tool, social media presents a shift in thinking from the days of direct marketing and one-way communication. Instead, social media creates a different opportunity to interact with potential clients and to build rapport with a savvier customer base. In the days of print, TV, and radio, there was only one-way communication with potential customers. There was no place to have a two-way conversation that built relationships and encouraged dialogue. The costs were high for a direct marketing campaign and the return on investment was low – usually lower than ½ of 1 percent. It was a top down marketing strategy that relied on brand recall and sales driven content, strictly controlled by marketing. The distribution net was cast wide, based on demographic buying patterns.

Social media creates not only information on demand for new and potential customers, but it also provides the opportunity for customers to group themselves based on their buying behaviors. No longer can marketing departments develop material and toss it out in the wind to spread and take seed. Now, they must listen to their customer base, interact on a more grassroots level, and develop relationships.

Marketing is often as important to the customer as it is to the business. Companies that are readily accessible to the consumer succeed in any economy. Finding inexpensive mediums for promoting easy access to a company is critical to companies trying to thrive in a global economy.

Social media is accessible to anyone with a link to the web and is an incredibly effective way to attract more customers and to educate them about your brand. The potentially great reach also means you are better prepared to handle the traffic volume you will get back in return.

Social media is good for business because it:

- Builds brand recognition and awareness
- Drives traffic to your website
- Builds and strengthens community

With all the benefits of using social media to gain attention, improve web traffic, grow marketing lists, and build community why do so many businesses avoid social media marketing like the plague? Fear. Fear of the unknown and the unfamiliar territory.

Fear of Social Media

Many companies avoid having any presence on social media sites because they fear that they will lose control of their message. If they allow their employees to communicate online with customers, outside of email, the companies feel as if they have lost control. They fail to acknowledge that regardless of their position, someone somewhere is talking about their goods and their services on the web.

Some companies prefer to ignore what is said about them on blogs, forums, Twitter, etc. They take a 'bury their heads in the sand' approach to social media. Instead of investing in the real time experience of their customers online, they spend exorbitant amounts on spamming their customer base with direct marketing, radio, T.V., yellow pages, and the perennial money suck: Tradeshows.

More than 25% of U.S. held businesses block social media access to their employees at work. Some, like mortgage and investment industries, forbid their employees from having even a personal presence on any form of social media, even in their off hours! They fear compliance issues, with the comments of their employees resulting in lawsuits against the company. So these companies block YouTube, Facebook, Twitter, LinkedIn, etc. They are paralyzed by the fear that an employee might say the wrong thing.

Most companies perceive little value in social media and fear that any time spent on these sites will cause a drain on productivity. Many companies see social media interaction as a security issue. They worry that allowing access to a public company profile could result in a breach of the firewall. Some are concerned that company secrets might be revealed or that an employee's tweet or post might say something that harms the company's brand image. Others worry that the use of social media websites will clog precious bandwidth. Even if these sites are blocked, tech-savvy employees will find a way to access them via proxy servers. There is always someone out there that is smarter than the machine.

Benefits of Social Media

The benefits of social media far outweigh the risks. With a few simple systems in place, a company can easily manage their employees and their brand image online. Some of the advantages of having a presence on various sites are that you can:

- Easily identify posts related to your brand.
- Monitor specific keywords.
- Analyze any conversations related to you or your industry.
- Find new sites to target with your message.
- Measure what content makes an impact on your intended audience.
- Follow others in your industry and create a dialogue to gain insight into industry trends and what your competition is/is not doing.
- Uncover new issues your customer base is experiencing.
- Uncover unfavorable experiences with your goods or services that you can address immediately.

Social media is also a great way to study new target audiences and explore if there is a good "fit" for your brand. Think of it as an inexpensive test bed to try out new marketing ideas, pitch a product idea, or conduct a simple survey. Customer feedback is a powerful development tool. The immediacy of the feedback that is possible on the web makes social media one of the most efficient marketing analysis tools currently at your disposal.

Case Example: *Karen Klein, C.E.O. of Silver Planet (www.Twitter.com/silverplanet) hired a social media intern from their demographic, using a social media job posting. Their intern's job is to help develop their corporate message and to communicate* *it with other networks. They wanted their web savvy seniors and their advocates for seniors to help them share their message and support their efforts. Klein knew it was critical to have as broad a reach as possible and social media was a powerful resource to do just that.*

> ***Tip:*** Social media exposure is measurable with real metrics that produce real information. You can measure:
>
> - number of page views
> - number of clicks
> - frequency of visits
> - number of returning visitors

Social media creates marketing possibilities that many companies previously could not otherwise afford. Social media provides an affordable platform for deep customer research. It allows even the solo-preneur to beta test marketing strategies within their niche to help them define and target a specific audience.

Reasons Social Media Marketing Fails

Those that give up quickly on social media marketing fail to see it as a community building effort that takes time and commitment. Social media marketing efforts often fail because there is a perception that it cannot align with company culture or that they won't be able to control their online presence if an employee decides to go "rogue."

Just like working on the showroom floor with customers or interacting with clients in a casual public setting, the same rules of communication apply. Social media interactions online are no different and good manners are still the companies' responsibility, regardless of the setting.

A New Way to Meet, Be Rude, and Really Annoy People

Social media is no longer just a way to meet new friends and to stay in touch with old ones. It is a way to create real relationships, conduct real conversations and work for the common good of the community at large. Keep in mind that every entry in social media is a digital signature of you. It is a permanent reflection of you or your brand/business.

> ***Tips:*** Here are a few simple rules to live in social media communities:
>
> - Avoid racial comments.
> - Avoid critical comments, ranting and raving.
> - Avoid abusive language.
> - Avoid foul language and inappropriate jokes.

"In the future, everyone will be anonymous for 15 minutes." ~ Anonymous

Be savvy and smart when online. It is imperative that you set and maintain clear boundaries of professionalism on social sites for your business. So many users online just don't get it. They create conversational traffic jams because they don't understand the rules of social engagement. They abuse the social tools and then throw their hands up in dismay when their accounts get shut down, get chastised by their community, or are unsuccessful as a business.

Play nice with others and they will play nice with you. Don't be annoying or belligerent. Just keep in mind that social media is all about building relationships. Be transparent and build real relationships based on giving and trust.

Making Social Media Marketing Work

How a business or organization embraces social media often determines their level of success. When customers and employees begin to spread a marketing message on forums such as blogs, Twitter, Facebook, video, and customer review sites; discussion shapes the message. If the message is positioned right, it becomes viral and takes off like wildfire. Today's customers do not make purchasing decisions based on pushy print and TV/radio advertising. Instead, they look to the web for reviews and information because they prefer to make an informed buying decision. You can no longer afford to ignore the power of the social web!

> **Tips:** What works best to build a brand online is to provide:
>
> - Information on your website and on social sites that people want to share
> - Opportunity for customers to generate content in the form of reviews, shared experiences, etc
> - Possibilities for blogs, forums, and social bookmarking of your site and your discussions

Social media marketing works best when there is input from the decision makers. When decision makers see the relationship between company goals/objectives, as well as the way that social media drives measurable results to that end; they usually "get it." Recognizing that social media marketing is not a campaign with a start and end date, but that it has a long term objective of building relationships and creating customer retention and satisfaction. This is critical to making social media marketing work.

Social Media is a great place to create and engage in meaningful conversations. Offer something of value to your community and they will continue to return as they come to respect you as an authority out in the "trenches".

Leveraging social media as a marketing tool is about brand building, establishing thought leadership, and customer retention. It can also be a great lead generation tool, as well as a resource for research and development of new goods and services. Social media is the fastest, least expensive method to announce the launch of a new product or service to your customer base. From crisis management to demonstrating thought leadership to your niche, social media is a forceful tool that not only spreads your message, but also helps you to be transparent, earn the trust of your community and to build credibility. With social media, small businesses have a real opportunity for huge growth of their Internet presence.

The effect on the business world of the Internet revolution is that anyone can now have a competitive edge, but only if they attempt to understand and implement social media. Social media now gives the consumer the means to participate and connect with companies, like never before in commerce history. By participating in the market place conversations, businesses that interact with the consumers and really take the time to listen to what is being said about them and to them, can't help but be successful.

Case Example: *Mom Blogger Heather Armstrong, known as Dooce on Twitter (www.twitter.com/Dooce) and on her highly successful blog, recently purchased an expensive washer and dryer from Maytag. The washer broke and apparently, so did the service plan, customer service, and the repair chain at Maytag. Dooce was not happy with the lack of customer service and the inefficient methods they used to provide parts and services to repair teams. Dooce used Twitter and her blog to first voice, and then to chronicle her frustrations; she informs her followers not to buy Maytag products. She used her celebrity to not only solve a personal problem, but she also called attention to the fact that Maytag's customer service was* *not customer oriented. She ultimately got her machine repaired and raised enough attention to her problems that Maytag's competition offered to help her resolve her washing machine dilemma.*

Marketing Success is no longer measured by how far your reach is, but by how deep your network is...how deep is yours?

Chapter 1: Twitter: Not Just What You Had For Breakfast Anymore!

Twitter, LinkedIn, Facebook, Social Bookmarking, and Blogs are powerful social media tools. Twitter is by far the one that currently gets the greatest discussion around the water cooler and is the most misunderstood by the public at large. So what is Twitter and why should a business owner bother with the darn thing?

Twitter is an online 'short-wave radio station', where a mixture of give-and-take chitchat, socializing and sharing of information transpires. What makes Twitter attractive to small business marketers is its immediate accessibility. The moment a message is put in the system, it instantaneously shows up in your feed. The fact that anyone and everyone are accessible (if they make their profile unrestricted), makes for a powerful marketing tool.

Microblogging on platforms like Twitter is quick, easy, and inexpensive (free) compared to a blog post, which can take a great deal of time. A Twitter "tweet" (message) is 140 characters and only takes a few seconds. A blog post, by comparison, can run over 150 words and can take a few hours to polish, in some cases. Because Twitter is so short, the message has to be clear, concise and highly targeted. If done right, Twitter can build loyalty that enhances your brand and recognition.

The immediacy of Twitter and its intimate nature helps you build rapport with your market rapidly with small messages. Twitter's great potential lies in its ability to act as a broadcasting tool and for relationship building within a community. It takes a different approach and some unique tools to make it useful for your business, but it is a great resource for promoting your company, increasing your online visibility, and creating a buzz that can be picked up by search engines.

Why Businesses Should Use Twitter

Twitter is a great place to create and engage in useful, meaningful conversations that can lead to sales leads, referrals, and so much more. In order to take advantage of Twitter, it helps to first understand a little bit about the demographics of those on Twitter in order to begin to see its potential for your business. Business owners are more likely to use Twitter than anyone else because it helps a company to quickly and publicly position themselves as an industry leader. It establishes their online credibility.

Twitter was tried by the teen/college crowd and was quickly abandoned by them. The average age for Twitter is the 35+ user. They are the ones out there in the trenches using social media as a large part of their business marketing plan. According to recent research, there is a direct relationship between how long a marketer has been using social media and how much time they dedicate per week to social media marketing for their brand. The longer they have been there...the greater the time they commit to the process.

Twitters Multiple Business Uses

Twitter can be used for marketing or as a public relations channel, to share ideas or communicate with your customers, to do market research and to increase search engine optimization (SEO). Often, your tweets will appear higher in search results than your company web page, so make sure your page is branded properly.

Twitter is a great conduit to see who is talking about you, your brand, and your competitors. It is a solid PR channel and resource for conducting market research and to monitor events you are hosting. Twitter can be a means for publishing a link to a survey or to gather answers to a question. It is also a great way to decide where to make your next investment in product development. As a listening post, Twitter is invaluable in taking the pulse of the public, to gather ideas, note behaviors, public opinion of your business/brand and to get a sense of what the latest trends are in your niche.

Case Example: *David Grigsby (www.Twitter.com/dgrigsby) of Grigsby Consulting in Carmel, Indiana – (www.grigsbyconsulting.com) uses Twitter as one of several resources for business prospecting. He uses social media as a news source and has found two types of Twitter users: me-formers and informers. Me-formers are just plain old gossipers. Informers share news. He found that the informers were more liberal in their tweeting and more useful. They will often leverage what you have to say, good or bad.*

David was skeptical about his reach with Twitter at first. But as he started posting daily, he found he actually got responses from unlikely sources. He began to use his daily status updates and those of his clients to pollinate his following in order to build trust and a reputation as a technology authority. David discovered that as he made people feel comfortable with the information he provided at a consistent frequency, they began to come to him with questions and to interact not only with him and his business, but also with other potential customers.

David found that there were some really important things to know or to uncover on Twitter in order to be successful. He needed to know:

- *Where do your customers cluster?*
- *What do they spend their time doing there?*

To find this information, he began to look at the status updates of his followers and those Twitter accounts he followed. He asked himself, "What is your intended result with your audience? Do you want them to laugh, learn, spend, or just be aware of your products?"

Tip: In order to be successful on Twitter it helps to have a good insight into what most long term users do on Twitter:

- Sign up with a unique Twitter name.
- Create a profile with hopefully their business or personal name, URL, interests (keywords).
- Develop a unique presence.
- Begin to develop a reputation as a Tweeter (contributor, spammer, influencer, etc).
- Invite their friends and acquaintances and sometimes their customers/clients from their personal and professional contact lists to follow on Twitter
- From groups they belong to such as Facebook, LinkedIn, Ning, etc.
- From attention they gather through business cards, newsletters, events, etc.
- Share information they find, know, and acquire.
- Collaborate with others through retweets, etc.
- Talk to other tweeters, first through direct message and often later through email.

Harnessing your followers on Twitter is your most valuable asset. You do that with your status updates and real one-on-one interaction with followers on Twitter or with email.

Twitter helps you create an informed strategy for your business. By observing what people do on Twitter, you can create a highly targeted social media marketing strategy that will have a high return on investment ROI.

Twitter is a powerful tool, despite or due to its 140 character limit. It lets you connect with your group, your "twibe" or "peeps," via your mobile device or your computer. It lets you stay connected to clients. It is also a terrific early warning system. Twitter allows relationships between people, who have similar interests and yet, they never have to trade a phone number or an email address.

A social network is the sum of its membership, so the platform the network resides on dictates how the membership interacts; however, it does not provide any real limitations for what you can accomplish on that platform.

Chapter 2: The Power of Twitter

Twitter is a great source of information and a great way to send out critical information rapidly for wide dissemination. You can quickly scan the Twitter stream for headlines and then only click over to the items that interest you. Because Twitter is 'real time' you can stay abreast of developing news on your computer or cell phone, and the information is the same, regardless of the device. So, if there is breaking news, it will get pushed to the world's Twitter feed.

Twitter in the News

In 2009, a terrorist attack in Mumbai, India left more than 85 people dead and more than 200 injured in multiple locations. Others were taken hostage by the terrorists. Twitter was the first place where eye witness reports began to appear. Twitter was suddenly thrust into the forefront as a resource for world journalists trying to uncover information about the events as they were unfolding! Unverified and at times fraught with mistakes, it was still raw and filled with extremely important first hand reports of the events as they happen.

Traditional mainstream media brings a reporter to an event, often hours after it happens, to interview participants and first hand observers and then, they must still verify sources, etc. This takes hours to accomplish before the content hits the 'news'. Twitter is there, it's live, and it captures events as they unfold. While not all the facts will be complete or correct, the participants will self-correct as the events play out and the information aggregates around the hashtags (a method of creating searchable metadata – think index titles - in Twitter) people create around an event.

The Mumbai attack used hashtags (#) in front of specific words in their messages so their messages could be indexed and searched on Twitter. They used the hashtags #Mumbai and #Mumbai #Massacre to spread the word about the murders to the world. Tweets came from across the street, from the café under attack, the hospital where victims were first treated, and others, who were spreading the word that Mumbai had a terrorist attack underway. It spread not only the news of the event like wildfire, but also the emotions of the people there and the reactions of those hearing about it around the world. No longer is it only traditional media sources, now citizen media is taking hold and benefitting the world.

One notable event recorded on Twitter in 2007 made a huge impact on a large metropolitan community. San Diego had a particularly difficult season that year with wildfires spreading and jumping fire lines. Evacuees used Twitter (and other tools on the Internet) to stay updated on information regarding their homes, the location of their loved ones, as well as to tell their stories. Specific hashtags were used for emergency coordination and disaster relief.

This experience led to many relief organizations recognizing the power of social media (especially Twitter) and led to more organized use at future disasters (as in Haiti and Chile). Collaborative efforts online are now a major benefit to relief agencies during natural disasters and civil unrest.

In the U.S. Presidential Election in 2008, Twitter played a large part in the Barack Obama election campaign efforts. Their use of social media to organize and engage voters was cutting edge and more sophisticated than previous national campaign efforts, thanks to the rapid expansion and adoption of social media by large numbers of people across multiple socio-economic groups. Add to that the use of mobile phones by so many young Web savvy voters, who were ripe for the picking. The Obama campaign machine even went so far as to create a free iPhone software application "Obama for America" that was built for users to organize their existing contacts by "key battleground states." Then the application was brilliantly promoted on Twitter.

Twitter was also used during this same presidential election to build viewership for the debates. They even had two official campaign representatives debate policy *on* Twitter. Liz Mair tweeted for the Republican McCain's viewpoint and Mike Nelson for Democratic Presidential candidate Obama. Neither were Twitter experts, but both were policy experts. The debate was scheduled to last five days and was slated to attract McCain's and Obama's more technically oriented followers.

The online debate format was not considered that successful politically or technically as it tried to distill political discourse into 140 characters or less per transmission. The organizers created a Web page to aggregate the Twitter posts of the moderators; however, they were still difficult to follow sound-bites. They used the hashtag #pdfdebate – Personal Democracy Forum. It may not have been that successful politically; however, it was a groundbreaking experiment for a national election in a social media forum that will influence the way elections are marketed to the nation in the future.

Even more fascinating is that candidate Obama had a Twitter profile that had thousands of followers. Neither Hilary Clinton nor John McCain had Twitter accounts. John McCain often laughed that he was so technically challenged that he did not even use email! As a matter of fact, the McCain campaign organization suspended a staffer who posted a YouTube link to a racially charged anti-Obama video from her Twitter account. The inappropriate use of Twitter as a conduit of hate and his own lack of understanding of personal computing made McCain and his camp seem out of touch with the majority of their younger constituents.

On the other hand, Obama's use of Twitter and his large following on it was a strong indicator of his grass roots popularity. He (and his staff) was able to capitalize on his online presence, not only to grow his online following, but also to raise funds. With the election over and the Tweeting Candidate sworn in, his tweets have stopped. Is this due to federal restrictions on presidential communications (The Presidential Records Act) or is he just too busy running a country to spend five minutes Tweeting? Would a sitting president's Tweets diminish the perception of the power of the position? It appears that the President and his social media staff have now devoted their efforts to 5 minute weekly YouTube videos cross posted on the White House Website's blog. The President's staff use social media's less restricted outlets like Facebook and YouTube posts videos and photos of everything from the family dog, press conferences, speeches, etc.

Considering that Twitter was so wildly successful for his campaign, it is interesting that the same techniques were not applied to informing the American people about the bailout packages or the health care proposal. Twitter seems like a logical resource for raising public awareness and addressing the issues, but neither political party appears to have formally taken advantage of the technology. It will be interesting to watch and see who else shifts their focus to the use of Twitter for strategically informing voters.

The three major parties in the U.K. closely monitored Obama's social media successes as they geared up for their own elections. Each party hired staff dedicated solely to social media and digital campaign efforts. Twitter's immediacy and direct delivery methods made it a key campaign element for reaching out to potential and existing supporters. It is also found to be a great resource for taking the 'pulse' of public opinion and to shape public perceptions. The Obama election machine had put social communication campaign strategies on the map.

Closed Societies and Twitter

The power of citizen media is a threat to those who fear free access to information. Nowhere has this been more evident than in the 2009 Iranian presidential election. The heavy handed shut down of text messaging and blocking of Facebook and YouTube by their government forced protestors onto Twitter. It became their lifeline to each other and to the outside world.

Citizens were reporting, in 140 characters or less, snippets of what was happening on the streets and alleys of Tehran as it happened. Those in Iran witnessed the protests and violent crackdown by the authorities, posted pictures and words of the massive demonstrations in the streets and on Tehran University campus on Twitter. Participants in the protests used Twitter to organize, evade the police/militia, and to check on the status of missing or hurt comrades. Twitter and #Iranelection and #iranrevolution had become such a huge conduit of information that the regularly scheduled maintenance of Twitter was postponed, so it would not interrupt the protestors' access.

Businesses need to be just as aware of the ability for user experiences related on Twitter to shape public perceptions as politicians. Perhaps more so! In the case of Maytag, they felt the wrath of one unhappy customer, who also happened to be a Mommy Blogger with a million plus Twitter following.

This controversial microblogging tool has become a powerful platform for many purposes. It is a great tool for creating viral interactive messages to share breaking news, get feedback or to 'crowd source' for quick answers. In many ways, it replaces text messaging for rapid on the spot 'reaching the masses' communication.

You are your message so make sure all of your messages jump out!

Paul Simon (@paulcontentman) - Sharper Content

Whether you choose to use it as an informal polling station, public address system, or sales and marketing center on occasion, Twitter can do all of that and more in an instant. This flexibility in service is what makes Twitter so dynamic.

Key Factors for Tweeting Effectively

Social media is a giant knowledge network of resources filled with people and information. The amazing thing about social networks, like Twitter, is that you can pose a question and get a rapid response. People love to help people and are usually eager to help those they believe are sincere and trustworthy.

Think of Twitter as the giant Internet water cooler. Gather round it for two to five minutes and hear snippets of gossip, have random encounters with interesting people, get exposed to new topics and ideas you might not have otherwise, and gain a better understanding of people in general. Keep in mind there are basically two types of users on Twitter: Personal Users or Professional Users. Just like people who gather 'round the water cooler....some talk about their kids and some talk about business or ideas.

Three Advantages of Twitter:

- Provides terrific insight into questions, concerns, etc.
- Generates traffic to your website.
- Great forum for spreading your brand, your ideas, and your message.

Some of the other great little extras you get with Twitter are that you see what people are saying about you, build solid promotions online, and even drive repeat customers to your business. Twitter is a microblogging tool that promotes people following people, brands and ideas as well as building relationships.

Twitter allows you to listen to the pulse of the world, so a wise business will at least plug in to hear what their market is interested in and talking about on a daily basis. There are too many users who use it only to "pimp" their wares and never take the time to listen, comment, or interact with their following. Those who merely sell, sell, sell fail to see the opportunities that Twitter offers them to be seen by their market as industry leaders and worthy of trust and respect.

Savvy businesses see Twitter as a knowledge management system to share links to white papers, informative videos, and slide presentations. Others use it to reach their employees quickly, like an emergency broadcast system. Microblogging is a moving target that shifts and changes to meet your needs. It is the sum total of what *you* shape it to deliver. Pay attention and stay engaged!

Businesses That Tweet Well

There are some businesses on Twitter that do a decent job. They 'get' that Twitter can be used as a useful tool for reaching current and perspective clients. The following companies may not tweet perfectly; however, they grasp the basic tenets of Social Media for business and appear to be making significant inroads with their followers:

Chevrolet: posts updates, interacts with car enthusiasts, company related news.

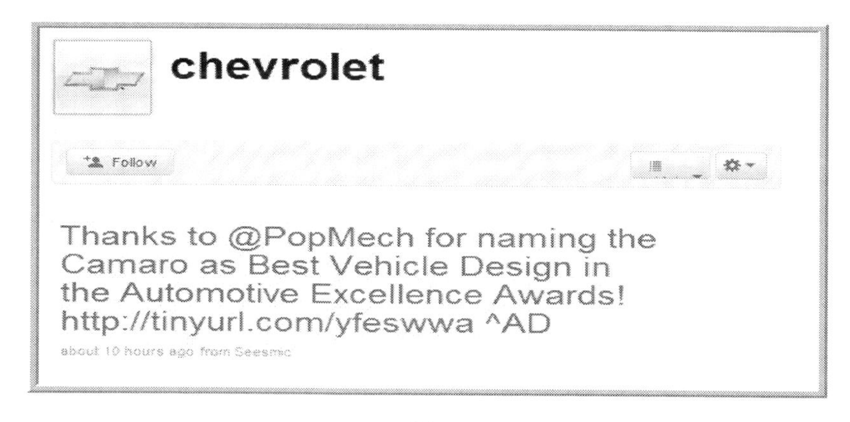

Jetblue: uses posts to stimulate customer feedback, interaction and discussion.

JETBLUE TWITTER PAGE

Alaska Airlines: works with customers, resolves issues, etc.

ALASKA AIRLINE TWITTER PAGE

Southwest Airlines: posts promotional fares, etc.

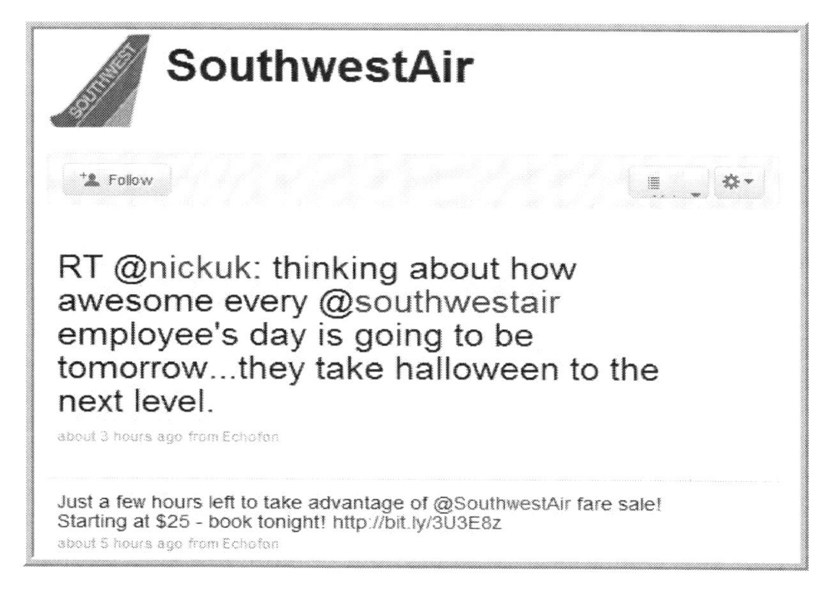

SOUTHWEST AIRLINES TWITTER PAGE

Harbour Pub: posts the day's special.

HARBOUR PUB TWITTER PAGE

Hotel 1000: posts specials, local events (Seattle), share information with guests (parking, menu, etc), promotes Seattle, local events, and hotel specials.

HOTEL1000 TWITTER PAGE

Chicago Bulls: provide injury updates, marketing, photo galleries, score updates, Q&A with coaches and players.

Smart companies pay attention and engage their customer base, wherever and whenever they might be. Customers are on Twitter to kill boredom when waiting in line at the airport, on the bus or train, or sitting in their dentist's office waiting room. Some people use Twitter as their instant messaging forum because they have instant access to their entire network via their cell phone, computer, netbook, etc. I have even seen a honey-do list come across Twitter between spouses!

Twitter gives people a reason to connect over similar interests. Since social media is about real online relationships and real conversations, what better tool to use to build community around a brand or an idea?

Northshire Books: local events, community news, sales, and maketing.

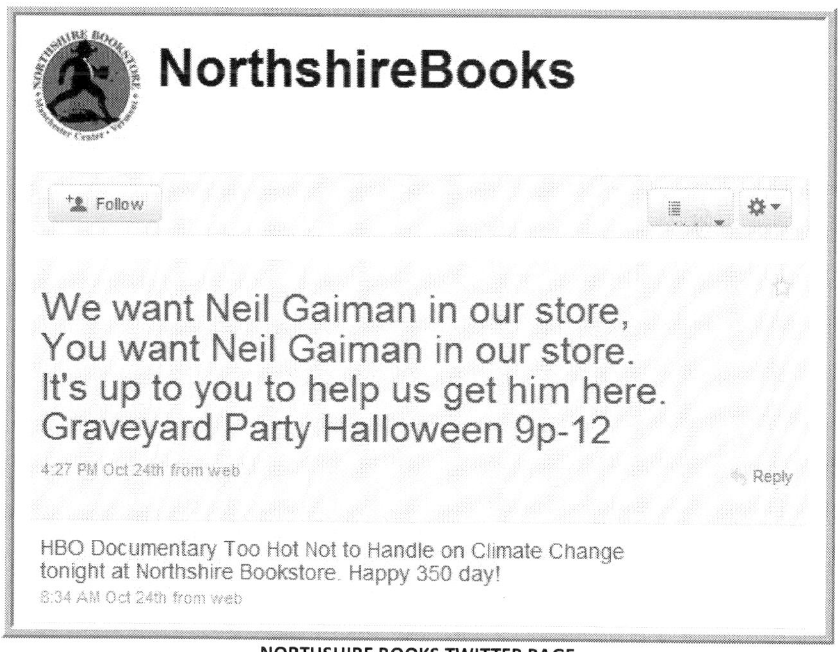

NORTHSHIRE BOOKS TWITTER PAGE

Twitter offers an incredibly unique method to listen to the pulse of the world and then quickly identify ways to enhance your business processes. It is a great way to share ideas, links, and make useful connections. Use it to network, market, and build your business. There are basically three ways to use Twitter: Broadcast, Listen, A combination of broadcasting and listening.

> ***Tips:*** Here are some ways to use Twitter today that will help build your following:
>
> - Be an expert on industry related subject matter.
> - Ask questions so you can learn from your audience.
> - Post industry related interesting facts, funny incidents, etc.

If you are an active participant and make a concerted effort to build new relationships you can't help but build your following. Leverage Twitter as another brand building tool in your tool belt. Use it to promote, announce news of success, as a customer reference resource, and even for professional networking. It is a free and highly effective tool for bringing new traffic to your website and your storefront. It is also a powerful way to get leads and generate new revenue.

Social media, in reality, is highly measurable on a massive scale. It is fun way to drive leads, promotes sales, and helps promote brands. It is more than just a place to hang out and deliver coffee quips.

The reality is that Twitter, the fastest growing social network, has over 14,000,000 users and is growing exponentially daily! Those kinds of numbers are telling. There is a huge market segment out there ready to hear from you and about your business. So get out there, be brief, be concise, and get in the global conversation.

Chapter 3: Getting Started: How to Create Your Account

Twitter can be a great tool. No, really! You can use it to build your customer base, stimulate conversation, conduct market research, provide customer service, and even post a coupon.

To create a Twitter account, simply go to www.Twitter.com and select the *Sign up now* button.

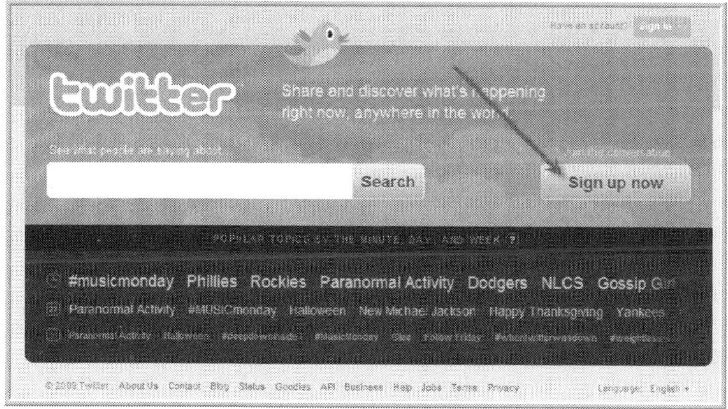

TWITTER "HOME" PAGE

You will first be required to fill in your name and create a user name (Twitter Handle). Create a name appropriate for your industry and your brand. Then you must create a unique password that is at least "6 characters and not a dictionary word or common name."

What's in a name?

Twitter names should be a combination of your top business keyword and a geographical tag. Twitter names such as @bellevuedentist, @austinrealestate and @syracusepetstore, if used actively at some point, may in fact provide an additional highly ranked placement in the search engines. There is a 15 character limit for your Twitter user name, so get creative.

Average Example:

Westseattleblog is rather a generic blogger name; however it has great local search engine optimization (SEO) 'juice'. Is the trade off for easy searching worth the anonymity? That would have to be weighed in the choice for naming the account.

Perhaps putting a "face" in the background that reveals the voice behind the account would help. As it stands the reader has no clue if the blogger is real or a machine 'bot'. Is it male or female? Who really is *Westseattleblog*? Will you be inclined to follow an enigma?

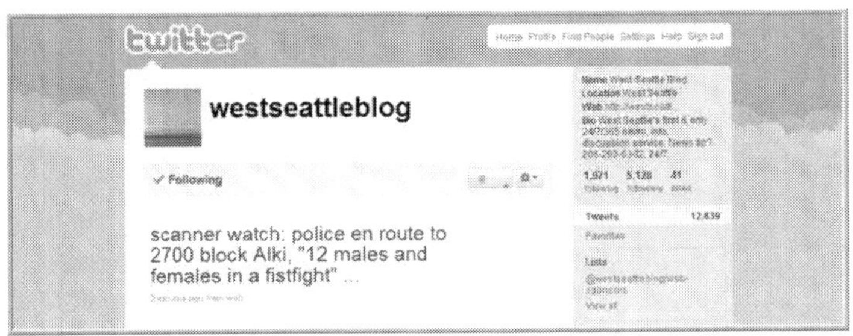

GOOD TWEETS BUT PERSON TWEETING IS NOT EVIDENT

Good Example:

Fantomaster has their business name for the Twitter account; however, it is really clear who is the "spokesperson" for the company, Ralph Tegtmeier. He also has a really cool background...more on that later...but note how he reveals who he is and his personality shines through too.

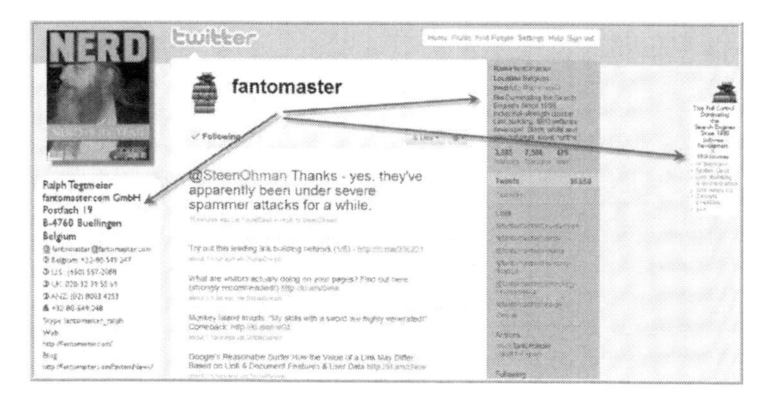

TWITTER BRANDED ACCOUNT EXAMPLE

Setting Up Your Twitter Page

Now that you have selected the perfect Twitter handle it is time to create the Twitter Page. Specify who is 'tweeting' for your account. If more than one person will maintain the account, use the initials to identify who sent each tweet in the Twitter stream.

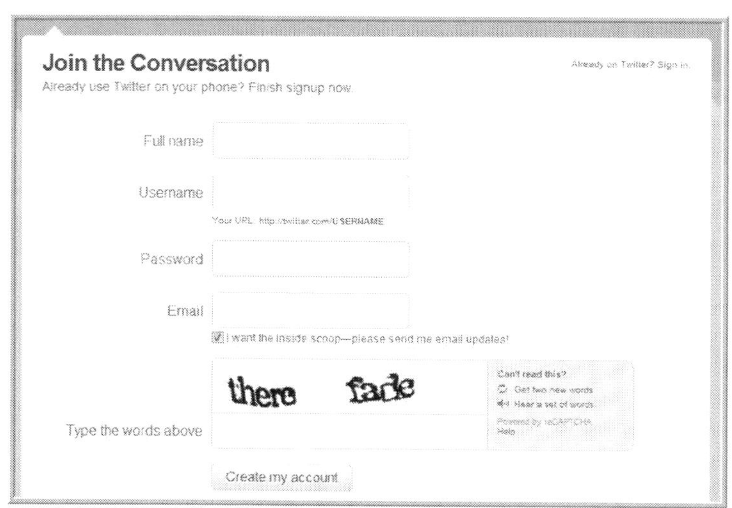

TWITTER SIGN UP PAGE

Once signed up, you will then be taken to two windows. The first asks if you wish to notify your email list on Gmail, Hotmail, and Yahoo of your new account. You can skip this step if you want. You will then be taken to a page with pre-selected for you to follow.

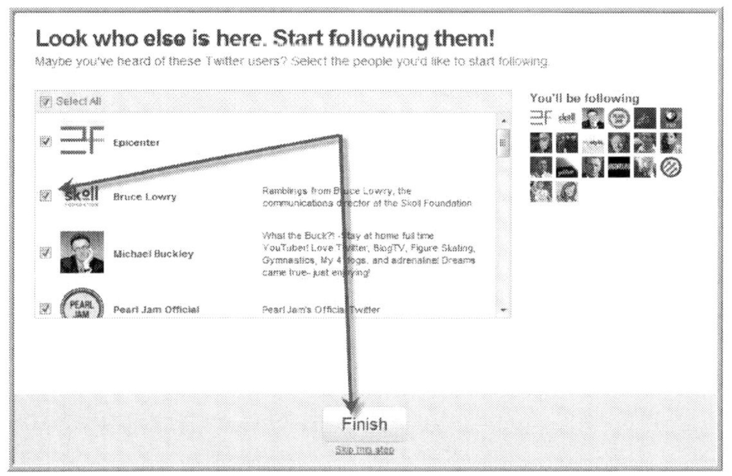

SUGGESTED FIRST ACCOUNTS TO FOLLOW

After you select "Finish" you are taken to your "Home" page. From here, you can begin to customize your page with a photo, branded wallpaper (background), and select keywords to help people find and connect with you.

The first step is to put in your photo also called an avatar. To do this you first select "Settings" from the top right of your home page.

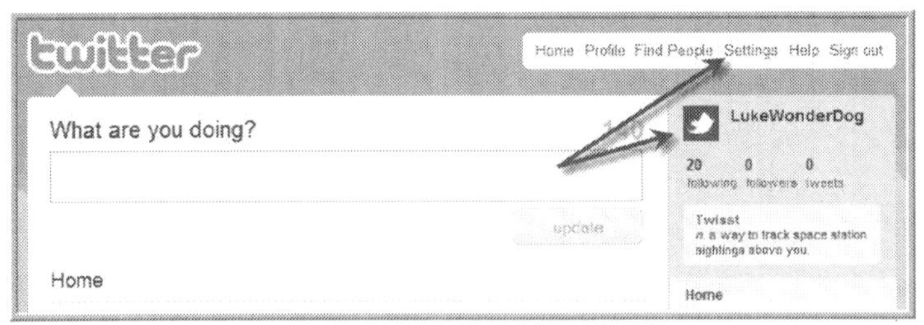

CHANGE AVATAR FROM "SETTINGS"

A new window pops open where you can insert your URL, your bio, upload your photo, etc. Select the picture tab.

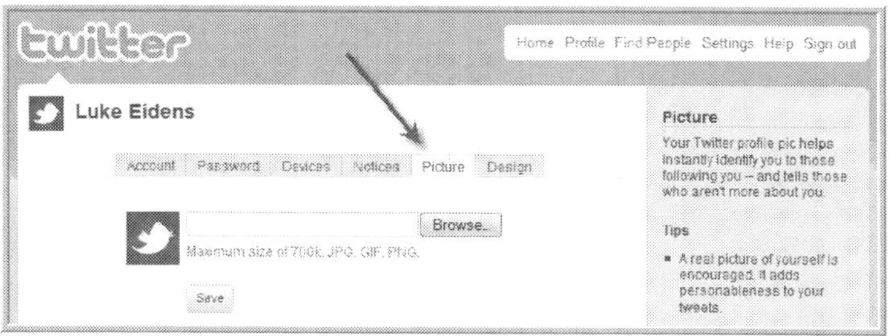

SELECT "PICTURE"

Profile Photo/Avatar: You will be taken to a screen that allows you to select a photo you have saved on your computer. It is limited by size definitions of a maximum of 700k in a jpg, gif, or png file. A small, compressed square photo works best.

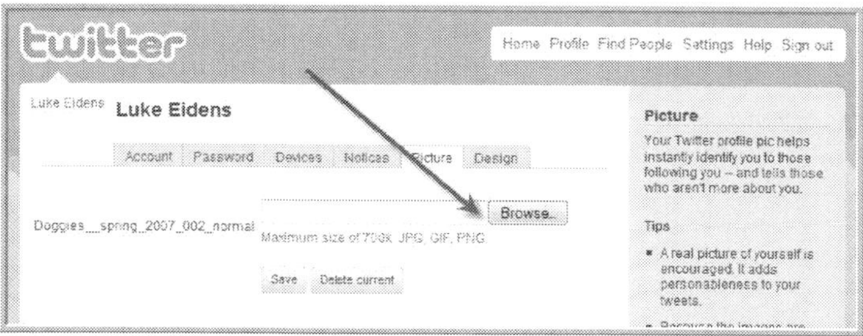

CLICK "BROWSE" TO USE AN IMAGE FROM YOUR FILES

Hopefully, you have a professional photo of you. Nothing bugs people more than a dreadful photo of you and the family at the Chicken Hawks home opener with everyone in their favorite player's magenta jersey! Impersonal logos are questionable as well, but not out of line, depending on the industry. People want to connect to you, instead of trying to "Disregard the man behind the curtain!"

BAD EXAMPLES:

NOT CLEAR WHO OR WHAT THIS ACCOUNT REPRESENTS

This is a stick figure that tells us no reason why we should accept that user is who she claims she is and represents. It may be a cute drawing, but is impersonal and gives the would-be follower no visual association with who the Tweeter really is or what business they represent.

POOR AVATAR CHOICE FOR A PROFESSIONAL IMAGE

While this guy might be a great Tweeter can his readers ever take his message seriously? This is really an amusing photo, but what does it mean? This photo really does not add anything to his personal or professional brand image.

GOOD EXAMPLE:

Reagan Hudgens, a travel writer, did a great job with her avatar. This is really her picture. It is friendly, open, and not embarrassing.

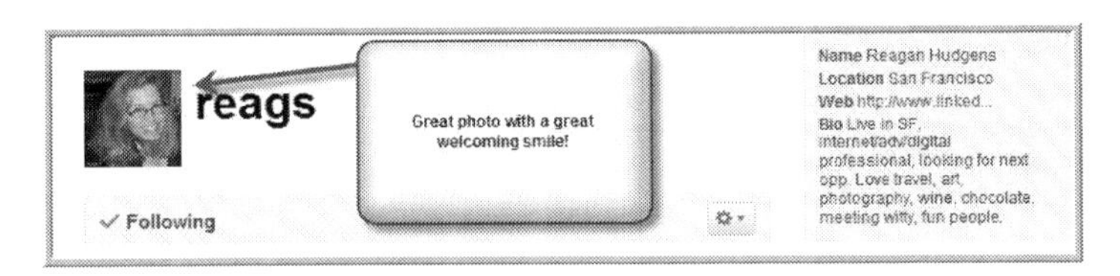

GOOD EXAMPLE OF AVATAR/PROFILE PHOTO

Andy Andrews, author of *The Noticer* and an inspirational speaker, has a great photo that captures his trademark smile (his profile would benefit from 'squaring' the image).

GOOD EXAMPLE OF AVATAR/PROFILE PHOTO

Once you choose the best photo for your site from your files, save it; and it will post to the page.

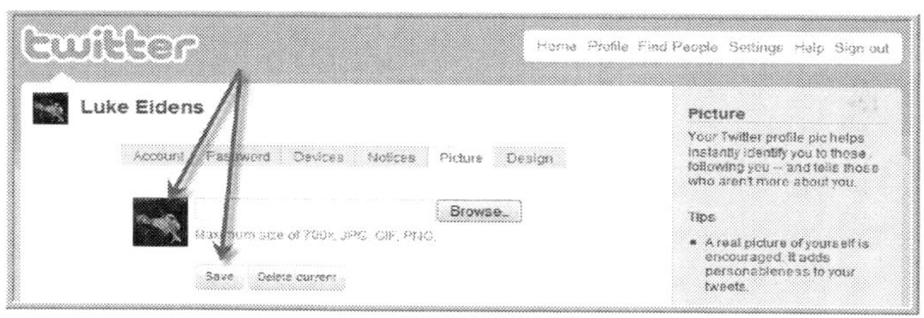

SELECT "SAVE"

Go back to the account settings and create the link to your website and keywords to use in a line bio:

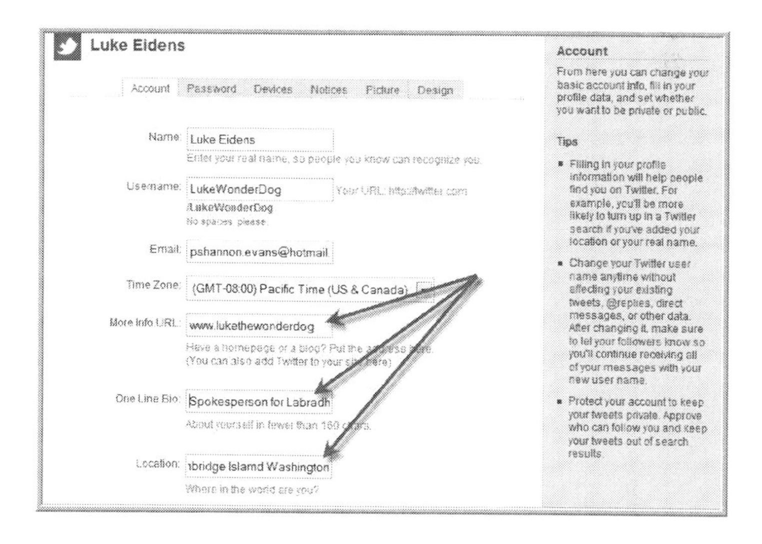

Website Link: You should have a website if you are in business. They are easy to build and inexpensive to maintain and host. Your website is where followers are going to go to find out more about you. If you only have 140 characters to communicate with your followers and they are hanging on your every word, don't you think they are going to go find out as much as possible about your company?

Some people post their Facebook fan page, others their LinkedIn page, but that is only leading your potential customers and clients to more social networks. You want them to go to your website and find out where you are physically located, what brands you carry, and what they can order from you online TODAY!

BAD EXAMPLES:

This person has no URL whatsoever.

PROFILE MISSING URL

The following person has a URL, but the link leads to a sales page for an affiliate site. If I want to know more about her, there is no way to click through to find out more. This makes this Twitter user appear heavy on sales and impersonal!

BAD URL EXAMPLE – URL LEADS TO A SALES PAGE

The link they post leads to a giant page online that is full of links and free offers that lead you off further down the path to a lengthy sales page:

CLASSLESS LANDING PAGE FROM URL IN A TWITTER PROFILE

The following example does not have a URL listed, but does give an email address…and a gmail (free) address at that! For a business that does not promote authenticity, it opens them up to spammers, who cruise the Internet to capture email addresses.

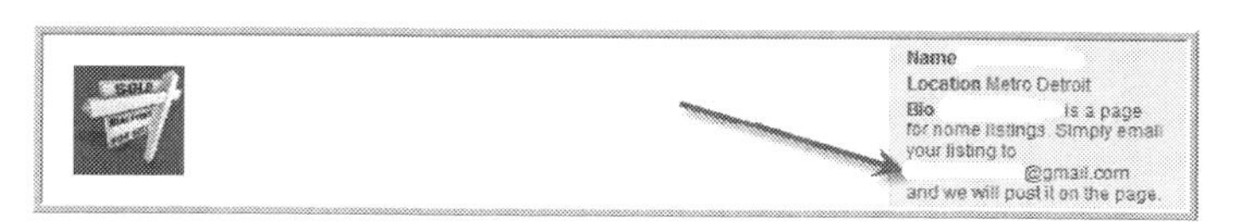

NON-PROFESSIONAL EMAIL ACCOUNT IN A BUSINESS PROFILE

GOOD EXAMPLES:

Non-profits tend to do this well:

EXAMPLE OF A BUSINESS RELATED URL IN NON-PROFIT PROFILE

Chapter 4: Customize and Optimize your Profile

Keywords are critical to getting you "found" on the web and especially on social media sites like Twitter. Keywords make you searchable by those who have never heard of you or your company.

The Internet runs on keywords, plain and simple. Understanding this helps you create an effective profile for your business. Who are you, what do you do, and what niche services or products do you focus on in your business? There are other important considerations as well. Misspellings can generate leads to your business as well. Different spellings of words can do the same. As an example, one of the most common alternate spellings of a typical search term is jewelry (jewellry). 'Jewellry' is the British English version of our "jewelry", and Twitter is a global social network...so take that into consideration as well.

Think like a consumer, select keywords and phrases that are heavily searched. Use tools like Google Keyword Tools or Google Insights to find the best words for your industry, products, or services. There is a 160 character limit on your description. Be sure to remember to make judicious use of your most effective keywords (including your location ones).

Twitter can be a great social media marketing tool for lead generation. There is the perception that Twitter and other forms of social media marketing are useless to a business because you can't really adequately measure the impact. There is a general overall belief that social media marketing has little to no impact on business; it is "fun" to play with, but has no relevance in the grand scheme of things.

Nothing could be farther from the truth! If you follow the right people you will be in the "know" in your industry you will probably be way ahead of the competition! Imagine if you had a resource for getting quick access to deliver links, increase awareness of your website, and create a new base of potential customers. What a fast and effective way to build a brand image! Twitter is actually faster than any other networking site at broadening your blog's reach and helping people to get to know, accept, and recognize you.

Twitter is a terrific place to create and engage in meaningful commercial activity. One of the easiest things to do to get started with Twitter for your business is to be a voyeur and explore the conversations around a keyword of your choosing. Use the search feature in Twitter to select a keyword that is important to you and your company. For example, let's assume that you are a mobile pet veterinarian. You want to find out what some of the search patterns of pet owners are and what services you might add to your business that will meet the needs of potential and existing customers. Think of some words and phrases that pet owners might use to talk about their needs?

Conducting a simple "related search" on Google can reveal additional search phrases you may not have previously considered. To conduct a Google related search first go to Google's search bar and enter your phrase ('pets and cats' has been used for the purpose of this example). Then select "More Search Tools" from the left hand navigation bar.

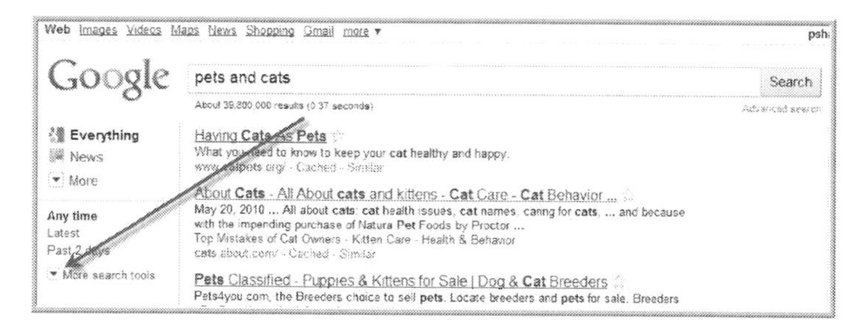

MORE SEARCH TOOLS

The navigation bar will expand and there will be a short list titled "Standard View", where you will then select "Related Searches".

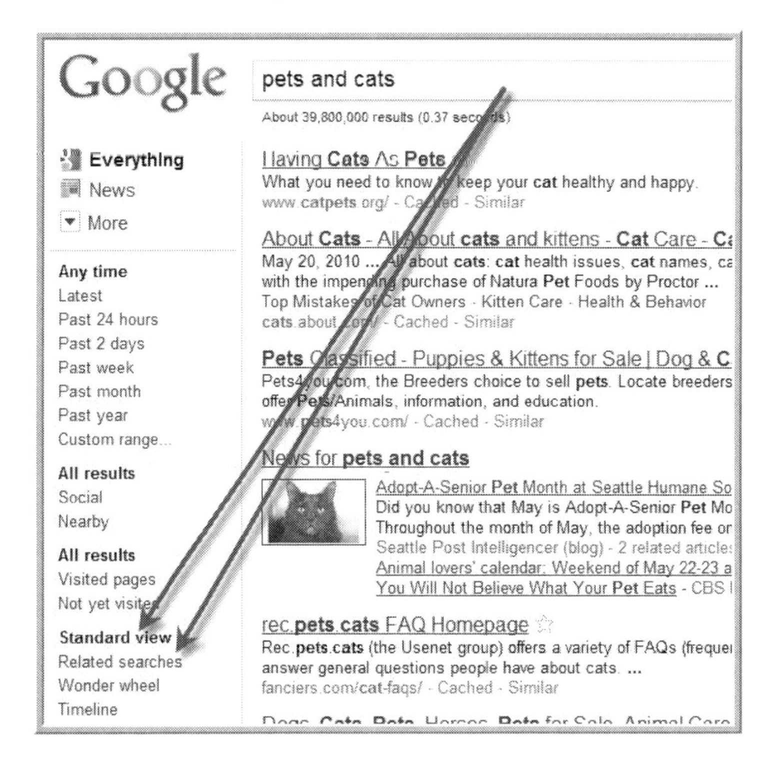

A simple Google related search for *Pets and Cats* reveals some words a person could use who wanted to know about how a cat might interact with other pets:

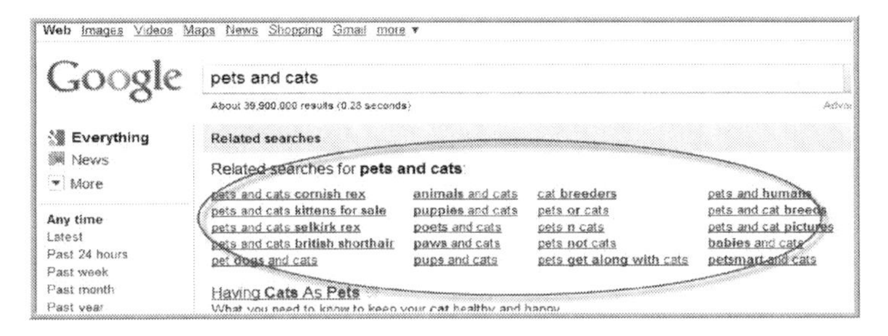

RELATED SEARCH RESULTS

The search phrase '*house calls for pets'* seems to be a popular search term in Google, so it stands to reason it might be a popular search term for Twitter.

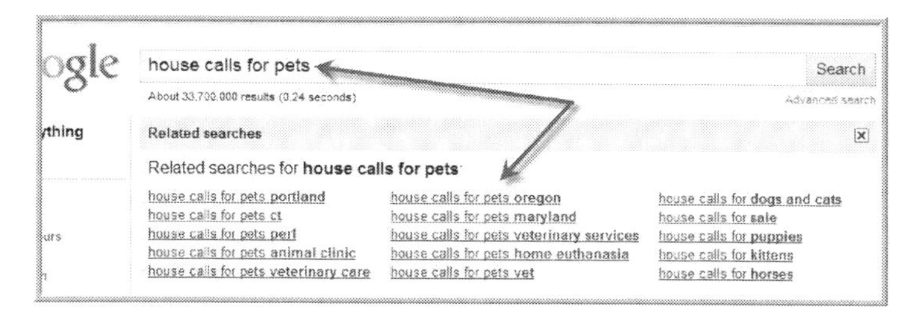

RELATED SEARCH RESULTS

Perhaps your specialty is horses and you want to be known for your understanding of common problems with horses. A commonly searched term according to Google Keyword Tool is "*lame horse*." Here are some related terms that might prove useful in your tweets and in your searches to reach and attract people who are horse owners:

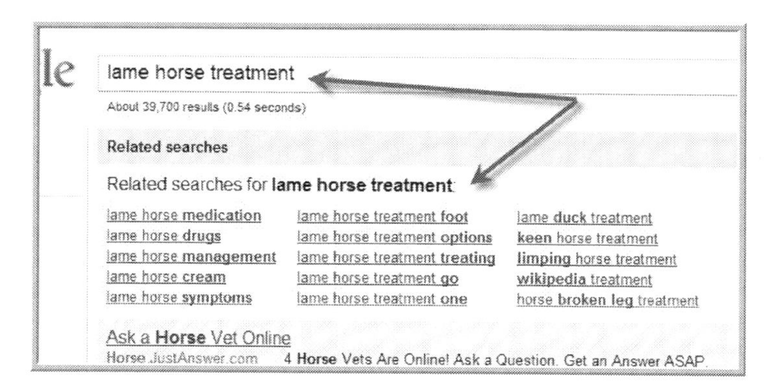

RELATED SEARCH RESULTS

Now that you have a good sense of keywords and phrases it is time to go on Twitter's search engine to find people who are using the same keywords as conversational phrases. Go to http://search.Twitter.com and select 'advanced search' just beneath the search bar:

TWITTER ADVANCED SEARCH FEATURE

Begin searching for people who are asking questions related to your keywords. For example, what kinds of questions and concerns would someone ask about a horse? What types of words would they use? If you want to cultivate a local presence you can even refine your search geographically:

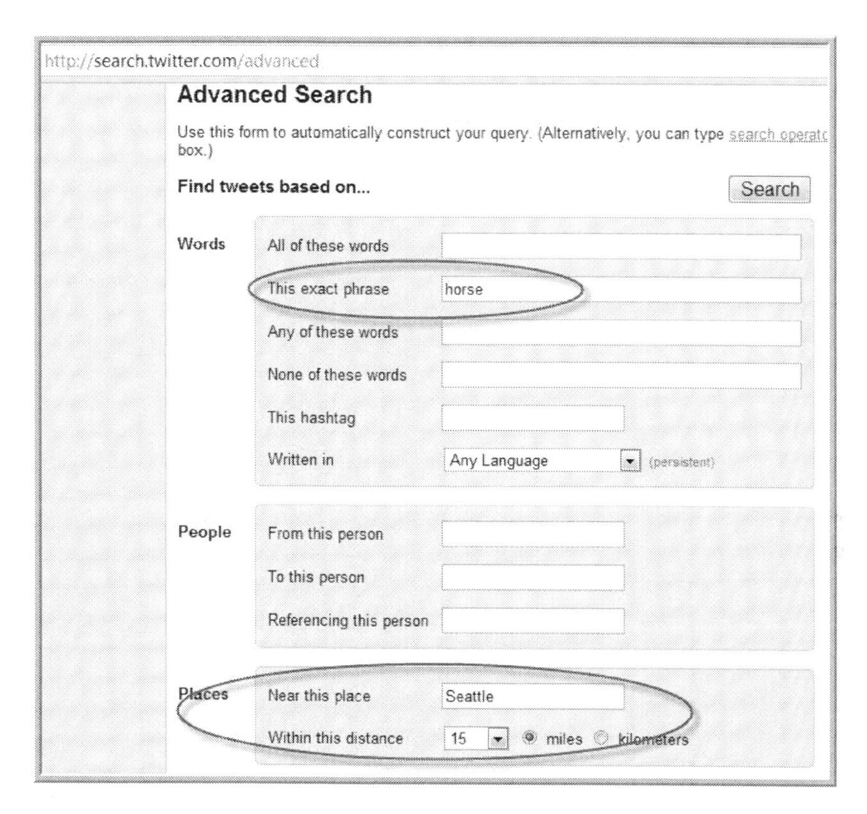

TWITTER ADVANCED SEARCH FEATURES

A really general search for 'horse' that was geo-targeted to Seattle revealed a woman whose horse has colic:

Notice that what is returned is a stream of a variety of conversations related to horses. Rather than spending tons of time scanning all the conversations to determine who to follow, whose profile to examine, and whose conversation to respond to or examine further you can see up an RSS feed using Google Reader as a content aggregator. RSS stands for "Really Simple Syndication" or "Rich Site Summary" and is nothing more than a way to subscribe to or submit content to subscribers. The RSS icon is found on the top right corner of the Twitter search results page:

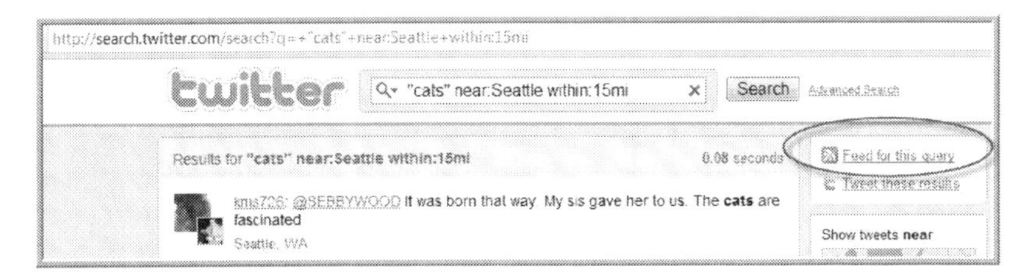

RSS FEED OPTION ON TWITTER

Right click on "Feed for this query". Select "copy this link address". You will then need to open your Google reader and select "add a subscription" from the left corner of the page. Paste the link in the browser bar that opens in order to start collecting your targeted search phrases from advance Twitter search.

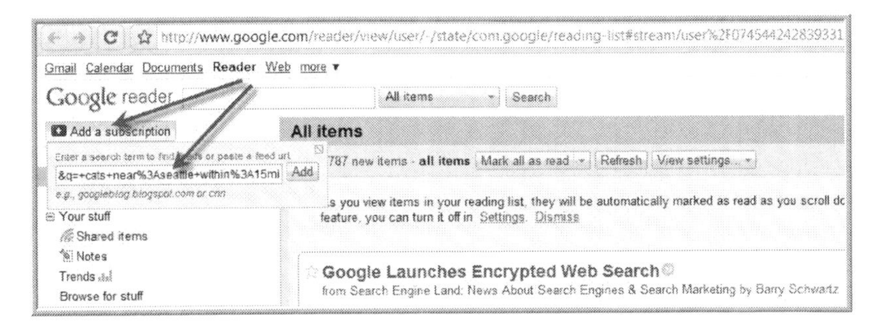

GOOGLE READER "ADD A SUBSCRIPTION"

You can also search Twitter using Google search. If you have goods and services targeted to dog owners you can use Google to search

Twitter profiles. First, go to Google.com and select "advanced search":

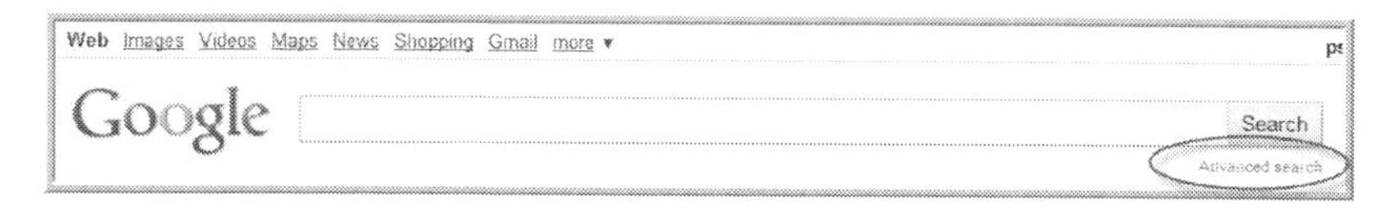

GOOGLE ADVANCED SEARCH

The advanced search page will open.

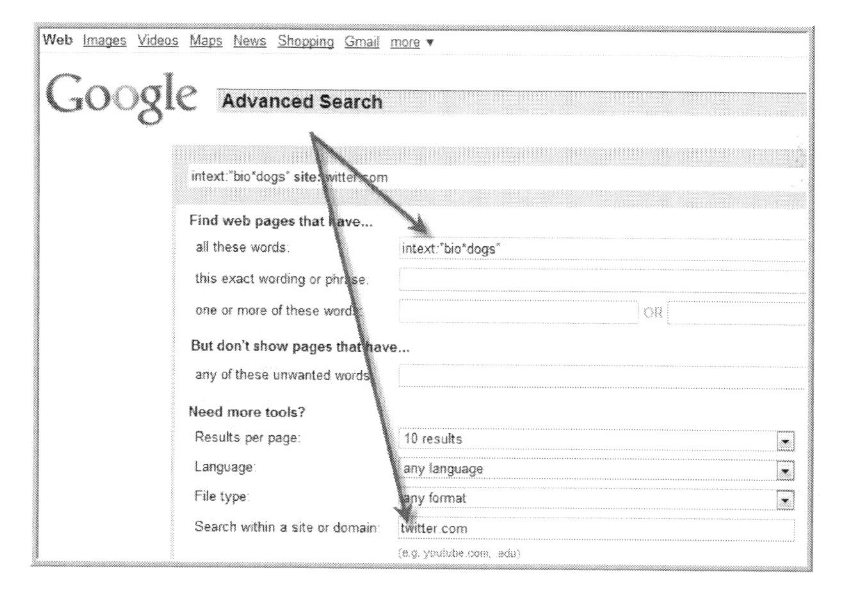

GOOGLE ADVANCED SEARCH OPTIONS

The first thing to enter is *intext:"bio*dogs",* then scroll to the bottom of the page and for the section "*search within a site or domain",* add Twitter.com. Using the specific line *intext:"bio*abcd"* directs Google to only search for text in each Twitter user's bio. You can also be more geographically targeted by adding to the "*all these words line*" a state or specific location *intext:"bio*dogs" intext:location* Seattle".*

Tip: Keep these social media marketing goals in mind when starting:

- Define targeted activity
- Engage influencers
- Share useful info, links to articles, blogs
- Establish a dialogue
- Identify social media marketing objectives
- Grow potential client/customer base
- Identify potential customer's unique needs in your niche market
- Share surveys and questions
- Post photo, video, audio links

Get in the habit of finding 5-10 people a day to check out and decide if you want to follow them and engage in conversation. Engage them in useful pertinent conversation first and then offer them something of value in the way of information, an article, a suggestion, etc. Once you start building relationships, the connections will grow and deepen. Show some signs of life and you will be thrilled by the outcome, as your reputation begins to grow with your following.

Once you understand how your customers find you on Twitter, it is time to focus on the use of those keywords. You will also find this to be a useful exercise in regards to a web site, if you have one (you do not need to have a website to have a Twitter account). It is important to consider any specialties you might have. While you want to capture as many followers as possible, the more specific your service or niche the better your chance of capturing the right following.

Do not use empty words like "mom" or "dad," unless your products or service specifically focus on other young parents. If you sell specialty bibs or one of a kind, environmentally friendly diapers for the urban hip parent…then you probably would include that you are a parent too. If you sell specialty handmade brief cases for men and women…leave out the parenting status. Don't use adjectives like "super" or "ultra" as they are wasted in the brevity of the 160 characters you get in the profile description form. Be as concise and accurate as possible, so you can attract a following that is pertinent to who you are and what you do.

Internet search is keyword-based; therefore in order to figure out what keywords are best for your business, you will need to take a few minutes and do a little research and some word play. The best tool for finding keywords is the Google Keyword Research Tool. This is found by searching in Google for "Google Keyword Tool".

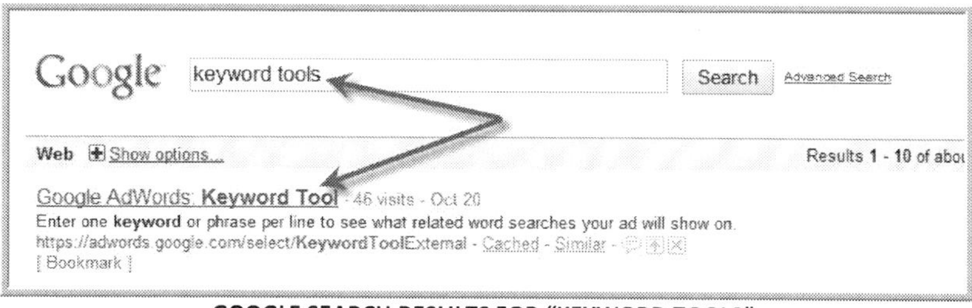

GOOGLE SEARCH RESULTS FOR "KEYWORD TOOLS"

Selecting "Google Adwords: Keyword tool" takes you to a new page. Google Keyword tool "home" page:

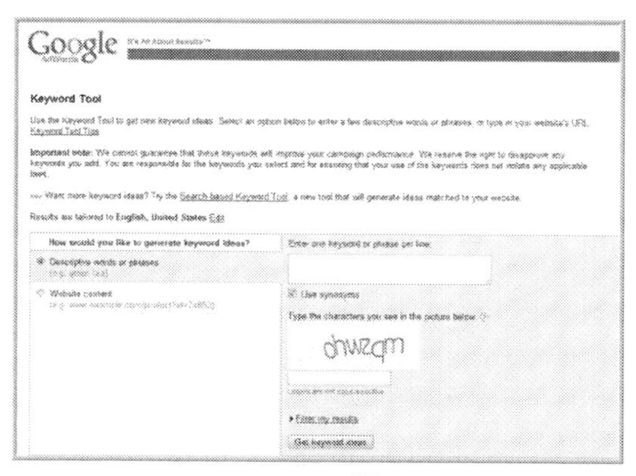

Enter your keyword to research in the box indicated and then type the characters in the window directly below the keyword entry box. This keyword should be what you believe is the number one keyword your customers/clients use to find you.

As you become more adept with this tool, use more than one at a time and see how the results stack up against each other. You may be surprised to find that other words are more popular than the ones you initially believed to be so.

A list will pop up with the word you researched and its ranking as well as associated words and phrases with their position ranking. In the example below, the phrase "local search" was researched.

Keywords	Advertiser Competition	Local Search Volume: July	Global Monthly Search Volume	Match Type: Broad
Keywords related to term(s) entered - sorted by relevance				
local search		110,000	110,000	Add
local search guide		Not enough data	91	Add
local search tool		1,000	1,000	Add
google local search		5,400	8,100	Add
local business search		3,600	2,900	Add
local search news		1,300	1,000	Add
local search tools		Not enough data	91	Add
mobile local search		590	590	Add
local search directory		Not enough data	590	Add
411 local search		Not enough data	170	Add
local search advertising		1,600	880	Add
local search marketing		4,400	3,600	Add
local phone search		Not enough data	480	Add
beyond411 local search		Not enough data	22	Add
ebay local search		Not enough data	170	Add
www local search		Not enough data	1,300	Add

GOOGLE KEYWORD TOOL RESULTS

First, jot down a list of descriptive words for your business. An example is provided here for 'local search':

local search, local search guide, google local search, local search advertising, local search marketing, etc.

Go through your list; select the highest ranked words that are closest in description to your business to add to your Twitter profile and to use later in some of your tweets.

Keyword in profile:

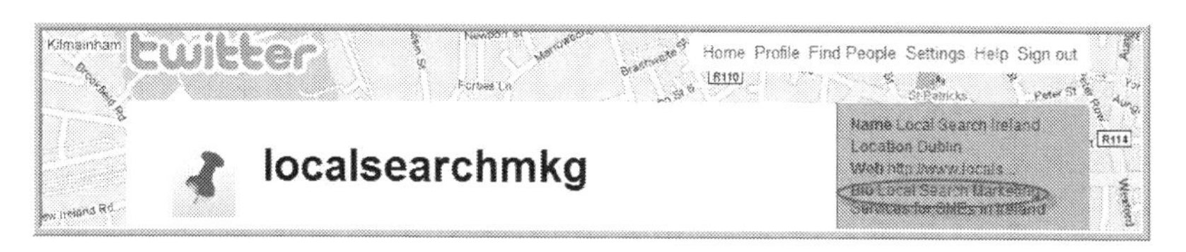

KEYWORDS IN TWITTER PROFILE

Keyword in Tweet:

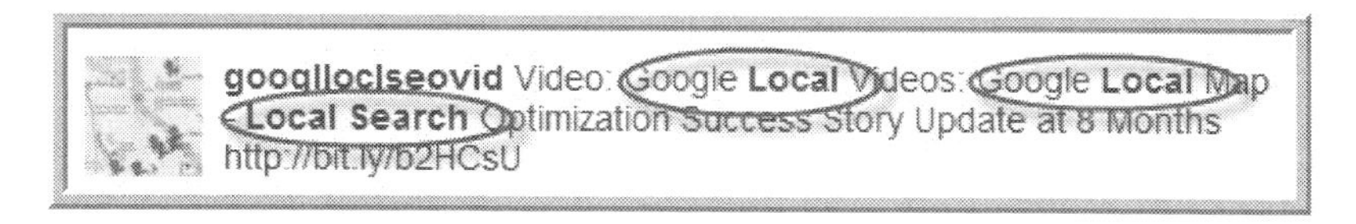

KEYWORDS USED IN INDIVIDUAL TWEETS

Twitter is really powerful for reinforcing your brand image. One of the best ways to quickly "brand" your Twitter profile is to change your account's background "wallpaper" and replace it with a custom one that represents your company. Use your logo, a photo of your storefront, or a label from your custom products.

Your profile is more than just your page, it is the portal through which potential customers, clients, and contacts first look into your business and your brand. If you don't do it effectively, you are missing opportunities to convert visitors into potential buyers and future business relationships. Your profile is equally as important a part of your marketing campaign for a company, as deciding which ad words to purchase! Your Twitter profile can make or break someone's first brand impression.

You can upload your own background images quickly and easily with Twitter. On Twitter you will see everything from the "cutesy tootsie" to the corporate button down, coat and tie look. Use your background to express your brand, your company character, and your personal expression.

Is it worth the little bit of extra time and effort it takes to create a custom background? Yes! There are millions of people on social media today and you need to standout in the crowd. A personalized background helps your potential followers understand and get to know you quickly.

Custom backgrounds also give you additional space beyond the 160 character bio to add more contact information. Having more contact information or more photos of you and your brand influences what the customer perception of who you are, and what you promote. When you seem real and tangible you are more likely to be followed.

There are some really great companies out there tweeting, who have really poor branding on their Twitter pages. The background is often blank and the information provided is almost misleading as to what they do well. There are other businesses that have great branded custom Twitter backgrounds. ENS a newswire service has a simple, clearly branded, easy to recognize Twitter page:

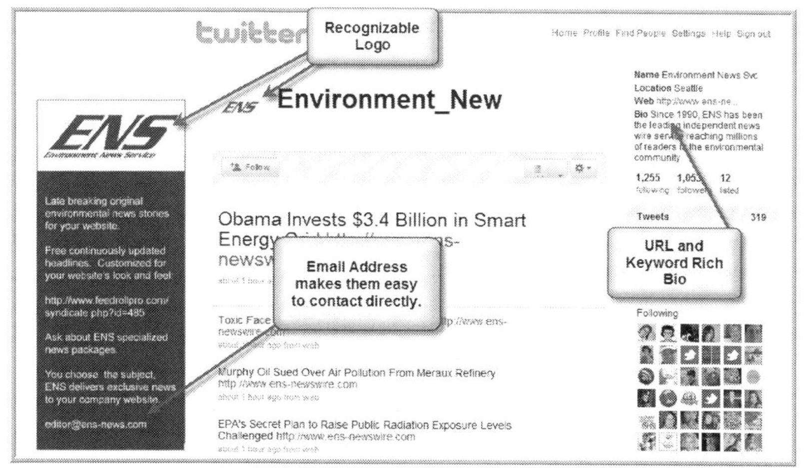

CUSTOMIZED TWITTER BACKGROUND

Customizing Your Background

So how do you get started creating an effective personalized branded Twitter background? Following is a list of useful Twitter design tools and resources to get you started creating your own wallpaper for your Twitter account. It also includes some great example designs that are cleverly branded, unique and just some of the most engaging Twitter backgrounds out there. Some have template backgrounds you can choose from and some have image editors to help you customize your background. There are really too many to feature here, but Twitter has many creative designers and users out there making great backgrounds. There is bound to be one that you can build that will be perfect for you!

Free Twitter Designer: free image editor specializing in background themes.

MyTweetSpace: lets users add graphics, text and create badges to update your background on Twitter.

TwitBacks: is great for creating left column backgrounds.

TwitterGallery: lots and lots of themes with color variation of themes that are categorized and are fast and easy to implement.

Peekr: a really cool bookmarking tool that lets you look at any Twitter background already in use on the Twittersphere.

Making Changes to a Twitter Profile

How do you get in Twitter and change what is there? Start by going to "settings" in the top right corner of your Twitter home page:

SELECT "SETTINGS" FROM PROFILE PAGE

A new window opens. Select the tab at the top of the page labeled "Design".

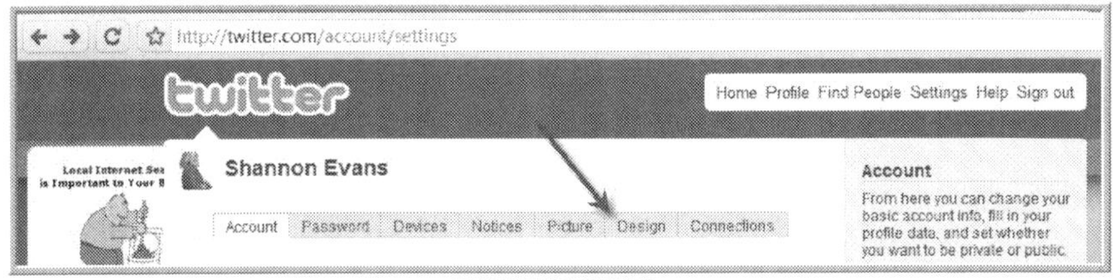

SELECT "DESIGN"

A new page opens with Twitter's standard backgrounds and colors, but at the bottom of the page are two boxes: Change background image and Change Color. For now, select "Change Background Image."

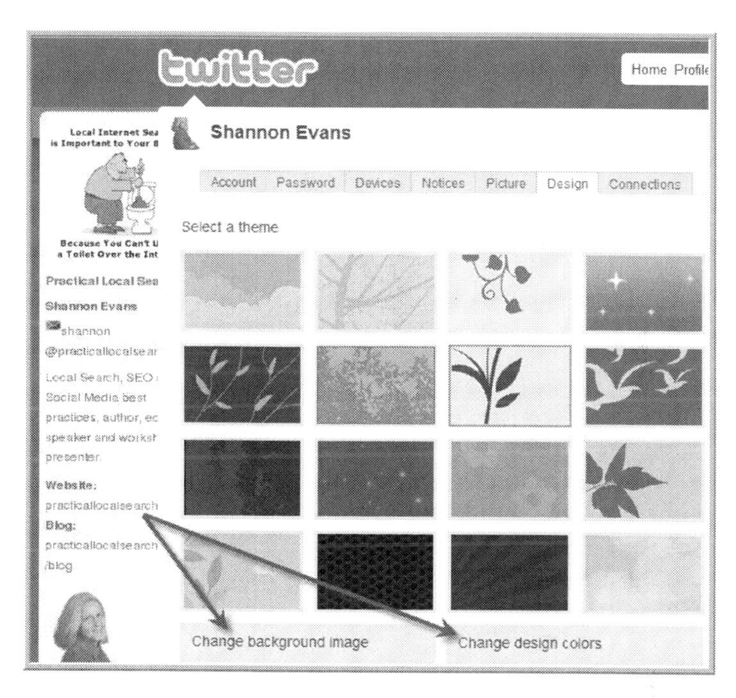

Now, you will be directed to browse image files on your computer. You can now upload your logo, your headshot, or any artwork you have designed and saved as a small jpg of 800K or smaller. You will be taken to your own internal files on your computer. I have separate directory for my photos. I keep my PR and Branding photos in a file labeled "PR".

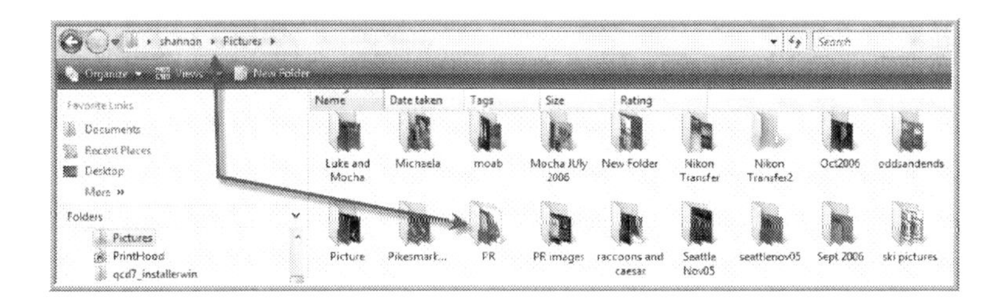

First check the dimensions of the images you want to use in your Twitter profile is important for intended effect. The total image size should be about 1600px wide by 1200 px tall so it will fit all screen resolutions. If you want to have one of the left hand columns that are becoming more and more prevalent on Twitter, make sure your images are 200 px wide (no greater than 235 px).

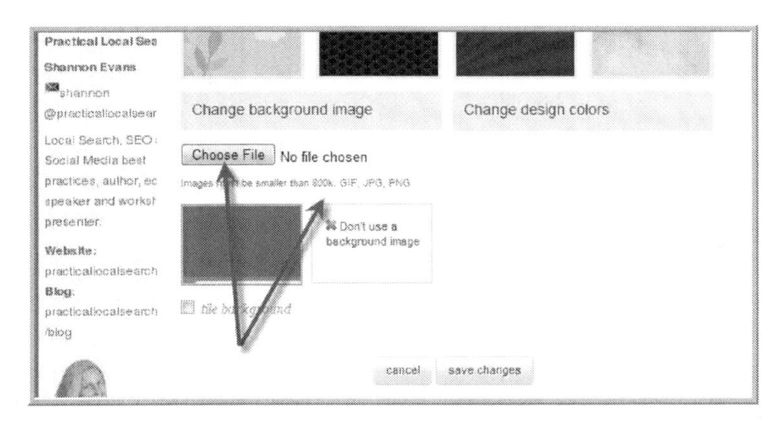

Once your profile page is customized double check it with an eye to the basic rules of marketing. Carefully review the wording both in your "bio" (biography) and what you included in your background on your Twitter profile. Check for consistency with your brand and your brand message. If you are trying to brand your site as an upscale auto dealerships specializing in high performance vehicles avoid the urge to include pictures of you and your cousins playing flag football and standing around a beer keg. Add fresh content as your business changes and grows. Post updates to your background.

Add your email, fax and phone numbers, website address, a link to your LinkedIn profile, etc. Give people options for reaching you.

Think "search engine optimization" (SEO) as you develop your profile and your background copy for search engines to crawl. Capture them quickly with carefully chosen keywords. People scan your page the first time they land on it to check you out. Branding your business originally took time and careful attention to detail. Give your Twitter profile the same attention you did to the initial branding efforts for your company and it will pay off. Follow these steps and you will have a Twitter profile that adds to your brand.

Chapter 5: Develop Your Following and Followers

The interesting thing about Twitter is that the more followers you have, the more popular you are perceived. Twitter is also a really reciprocal community. It is kind of like the Junior High/Middle School mentality, "If you will be my friend I will be your friend..."

Building a base of followers that are appropriate for profile building takes concentrated effort. The temptation at first is to get followers and to follow *everyone* back. Just like in any other social network, both online and in person, you want to be careful who you surround yourself with and who you 'hang out" with on a regular basis.

Pay close attention to the type of people who are following you and who you follow back. There are some who use "bots" to automatically pick and choose who they follow. They can be marketers, who shamelessly and endlessly self-promote or they can be pornographic spammers. You have to pay attention or you can end up with some "interesting" things showing up in your Twitter stream.

Here is how "Follow/follower" ("friending") works in Twitter: when you elect to follow someone, they get an email notifying him/her that you are following them (their updates).

Then, if they are smart Twitter users, they will decide on whether they will follow you back. How do they decide? Well, they might look at your current Tweets or your keywords in your profile. They will also look at your photo/avatar to see if you have one and what it represents. If there is only a blank box they probably won't follow without even looking at your content, keywords, or website. Nameless faceless boxes are usually spammers.

As you build and share more useful content in your Twitter stream, your following will begin to increase exponentially at first. With a little practice and selective cultivation you should be able to have at least 100 new followers a month. Resist the temptation to over follow or you will find yourself overwhelmed by what is sent to you in the Twitter stream.

So who do you want to follow and how do you decide who to follow back? I work in the world of social media, local search, and search engine optimization (SEO). I follow people in these fields, people with blogs that I follow on a regular basis, and experts in my niche. I also follow some of my personal friends and then a few who are just entertaining to me! I follow close to 6000 people (and growing), but believe it or not, it is still growing as I discover new interesting or noteworthy people to follow. And I keep many of them in lists (a way to organize groups of people according to categories you create), so I can keep them straight! Lists make it easier to monitor multiple conversations.

You want your follower to following ratio to be balanced. This helps you to avoid being perceived as a spammer. If the number you follow is significantly higher than your followers you run the risk of being seen as a spammer.

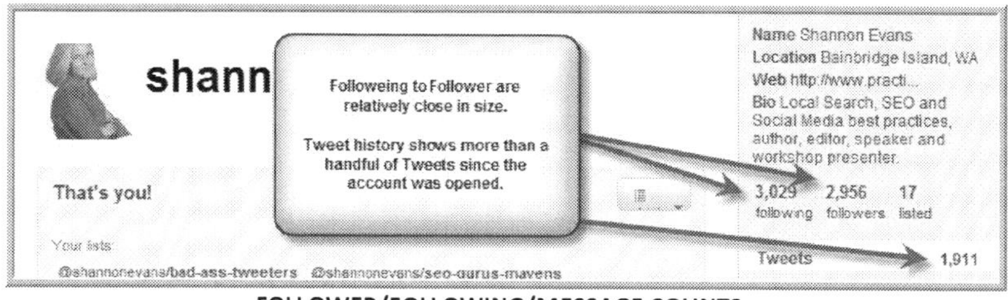

FOLLOWER/FOLLOWING/MESSAGE COUNTS

A spammer suspect has an incredibly high rate of follow to follower and only 10 tweets so far. Hmmm…and he is not a notable figure who is famous or infamous. This guy's ratio of followers to following and number of tweets screams "Spammer!"

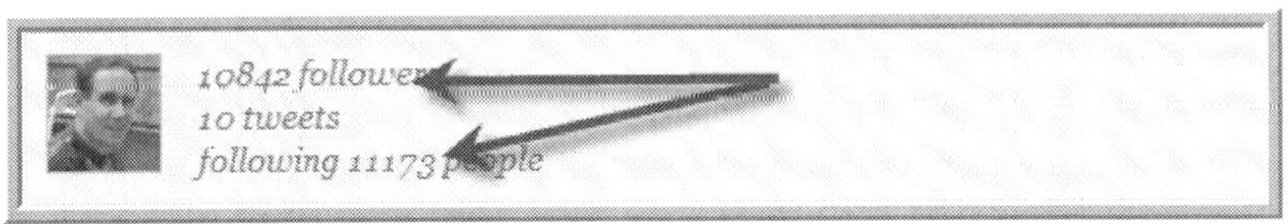

FOLLOWER TO FOLLOWING AND TWEET RATIO SCREAM "SPAMMER"

Grow your follower base slowly and let it grow more organically. You can build a rich and growing following with your existing community by putting a Twitter "Follow Me" badge on your blog, website, and on the bottom of your emails.

EMAIL SIGNATURE WITH TWITTER FOLLOW LINK

Next you must interact with your fellow Tweeters. Let people know you are there! Don't just follow people message them directly using the "@username" before the content. These are not private messages. These will be visible to all who follow you and anyone who visits your profile. These are highly targeted tweets that create a hyperlink of the @username you created. Here is a scenario demonstrating how to leverage a conversation. Assume that you followed @DivineMissM and she is a powerful mommy blogger for products and services that make life easier for parents. You ask her a question via Twitter. She answers it AND links back to your website. Now all her followers see that and many of them take that as a clue that they should follow you too! That is the power of Twitter networking! Your conversation is now even searchable on Twitter via the @username. Jason Pollock does this well:

"@USERNAME" EXAMPLE

Case Example: *Internet entrepreneur Larry Wentz (@LarryWentz) has developed a consistent and persistent manual method for building his following and cultivating conversations. He uses tools like Tweepi and WeFollow to identify people with similar interests to manually follow. If he looks at their tweets and they advertise "teeth whitening" or have suggestive photos and tweets he obviously does not follow them. Larry has found that manual follows make for a better quality of people and makes it easier to see who has the most followers and most recent 'real' conversations.*

Once Larry finds who is a prime person to follow, he then carefully selects from their followers. He looks primarily for people who are growing their accounts, have a profile that is inviting, have recent content, have a balance of fresh content and retweets (sharing a quote from another Twitter user), and have a balanced follower to following ratio.

Larry also looks in places where he would not personally follow back and often finds quality followers: new accounts. Sometimes you find good followers who, though new to Twitter, are eager to learn the ropes and share your material before they venture out to share their own.

Give, Share, and Be Helpful

Just like in real relationships with people in your personal network, you have to give and not just take. Give Twitter followers a reason to follow you. Don't be a spammer follower like these jokers who recently sent me the same DM:

DIRECT MESSAGE FROM A SPAMMER

DIRECT MESSAGE FROM A SPAMMER

Make you followers laugh, ask questions about them, and their passions, make yourself useful with interesting links and information. Add value to the Twitter stream with your input but if you have nothing noteworthy to say...it is best not to say anything!

Case Example: *Peter Chee, owner of Thinkspace, (www.Twitter.com/petechee), (http://thinkspace.com) (www.Twitter.com/thinkspace), is an ex-technologist turned co-working space entrepreneur in Seattle. When he first saw social media he thought to himself, "The Internet is going through another paradigm shift!" Peter saw the business potential of social media and how it would change how the average person would use technology. He has always been quick to adopt and embrace new social platforms and joined everything! Then he began to experience the fire hose effect of social media overload. He quickly learned he needed to change his approach.*

Peter was awe struck, "These are potential customers! How do I get in front of them?" He decided he needed to find where his 'peeps' hang out. Off he went to explore Twitter and its millions of different channels for communication. Initially, he talked about his company, Thinkspace's logo, and virtual offices. Then he started watching others who were successful on Twitter and saw they used Twitter with a personal touch. According to Peter, he had to get clear on:

- *Where is my business today?*
- *Where do I want it to be?*
- *What is currently missing from the equation?*
- *What do I have to do to change it?*

He began to follow different types of people and shared things that were not just Thinkspace related. Instead, he began to share things related to what Thinkspace is about: business and entrepreneurialism. Peter has concentrated Thinkspace's efforts on finding smart, energetic entrepreneurs who are interested in building a community that seeks to generate revenue. Since he changed his approach on Twitter to providing useful information that supports small businesses, Peter says, "People are talking to me directly!" The synergy and collaboration of entrepreneurs energizes his efforts. "What is really amazing about all this," adds Peter, "is that social capital is driving some of my financial capital. It is directly related to enlarging the sales funnel for many entrepreneurs I work with and talk to daily."

Peter made a point to establish a social media presence that helped him get clear on his goals for each social platform.

THINKSPACE'S BRANDED TWITTER PROFILE

It is no longer about the tool, but about the channel. This realization completely changed how Peter Chee and Thinkspace used technology to meet people. He now has a community manager, Alyssa Magnottie to help manage internal and external communication from www.Twitter.com/thinkspace.

Who will you follow and who do you want following you? Clarity in your Twitter community building goals and objectives only takes a moment and the results are truly amazing! Get focused and target quality over quantity.

Chapter 6: Start Tweeting

You joined Twitter, created a branded profile, posted a few messages, followed a few random people, and read some posts, now what do you do? You are set up and know who to follow on Twitter...what next? What do you say? How do you not get sucked into the black hole of talk, talk, talk? How do you avoid toxic people or toxic topics?

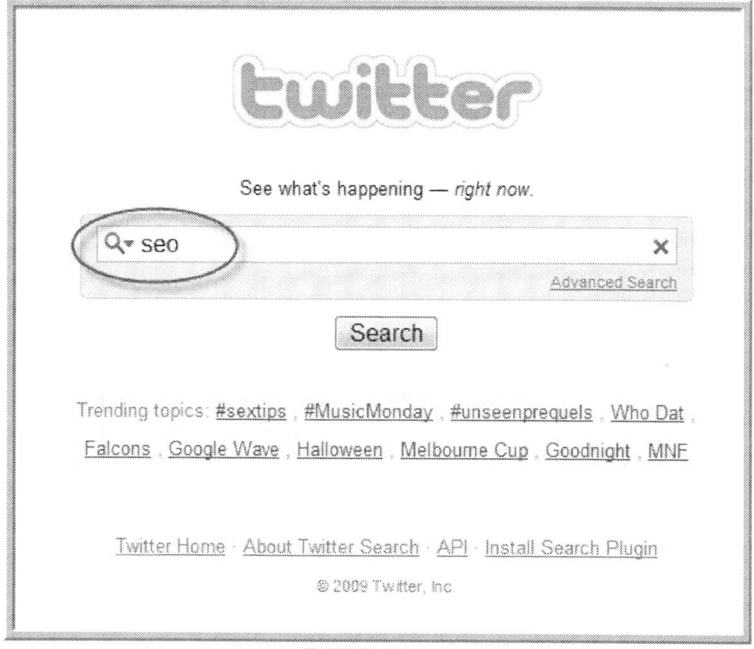

TWITTER SEARCH

Starting out on Twitter requires patience and a commitment to trial and error. Use search.Twitter.com to input keywords to find other similar brands products, or people who are interested in similar topics. Entering specific keywords or keyword phrases like "SEO" in Twitter advanced search reveals a bolded list of recent Tweets using that word or phrase.

TWITTER SEARCH RESULTS FOR "SEO"

There are other real-time search engines for Twitter. Tweetscan, Tweetzi, and TweetScan are some of the many applications that allow you to search Twitter for keywords and trending topics. Use these tools to help you find Twitter accounts to follow.

Follow and interact with people with similar interests, while you begin to establish your brand's presence. Ask questions, share information, request feedback, and get a conversation going. What can you do to get people to talk to you and about you? Spread ideas and make your content easy to find.

Share information, retweet, and even share some of their work on your company blog if appropriate. There is no one way to Tweet, but some standards and expectations are beginning to take shape. There are a few basic rules of engagement to keep in mind as you begin to tweet. The first is to focus on engaging in conversations with your followers and to not just push your products and your content. That can't be said often enough. If followers think they are being spammed or sold a package of goods, they will unfollow and block you faster than you can say Donald Trump has a bad hair piece! They might also Tweet negatively about you and your shameless self-promotion.

TWITTER USER RATTING OUT A SPAMMER

Engaging with others on Twitter can be a rewarding experience. It creates opportunities for exchanging ideas and entering into dialogues with people you may never have met otherwise.

Case Example: *Paul McFadden of Seattle started a whole new friendship just because of a comment about a book he was reading, The Go-Giver. Bob Burg, the book's co-author, began a dialogue with Paul on Twitter. As a result, they have created a genuine relationship. Paul states, "This made a real impression on me and on Bob; you need to be aware of what is being said about you on Twitter, but to you as well. If he had not been paying attention to discussions surrounding his book we probably would never have met!"*

Some Basics to Keep in Mind When Tweeting

Promote other people's content ten times more than you promote your own. Say good things that others in your industry (even your direct competitors) are doing. Share related links to articles, surveys, etc that would interest your followers:

Use @ replies to comment back to followers. Using the symbol '@' before a user name alerts them to the fact that you are responding to them dircctly in the public Twitter stream. This lets you tweet to someone and respond to them directly where others can "listen" too. In Twitter, this is a 'reply'.

Retweet: Retweeting is a great way to promote other Tweeter's content. Retweeting is when you take a Twitter message someone else has posted and send the same message out to your followers crediting the original author. Retweeting or RT's are good for the original poster, but also for the person who retweets. It builds goodwill between the original tweeter and the retweeter, and it exposes their tweets to a whole new audience.

Retweeting is where you copy and paste another user's post because you found it interesting and valuable enough to share with your followers. To ReTweet another user's message place

"RT@username" and then cut and paste the original Tweet after their name. In Twitter's api you can RT directly as it is found in the Twitterstream on your page in a highlighted 'button' on the bottom right of your screen. The original post will appear immediately after the RT @username. Retweeting adds value to your followers and brings a new dimension to sharing.

It is good Twitter etiquette to show that a message is a retweet. Always credit the original sender, and perhaps add a note to add relevance for your followers:

Retweet:@nameoforiginalsender Original Post. Helpful for XYZ.

Or

RT:@nameoforiginalsender Original Post. Helpful for XYZ.

If you share someone else's content credit them. To give credit where credit is due, you simply add RT and @reply syntax in front of the post. For instance:

GOOD RETWEET CREDIT EXAMPLE

Notice Calvin Lee (@mayhemstudios) includes not only the link from @greektyrant, but also the quick note about the link. Retweeting is really simple to do and adds to the community, making you not just a voyeur or self-promoting Tweeter, but showing that you see the value in sharing the content of others.

The basic concepts surrounding retweets are pretty simple and straight forward. RT's are not about promoting gossip or about back scratching, it is about sharing and cultivating a following of like-minded people.

Retweeting works best when you don't have an agenda and are authentically sharing posts that are interesting and relevant. While it does increase the likelihood of that person retweeting your material at a later date, that should not be the primary focus of RT's. A selective process of sharing good information with your followers is a better practice in the long run.

When you bring value to your following, you will not only keep existing followers, but will also attract new followers. When your followers begin to trust that you consistently bring beneficial links to the Twitter stream, you are more likely to get "click-thrus" to your own material, blog posts, etc.

A nice byproduct of retweeting is how it can help build relationships, especially with those whose material you felt was worthy of sharing. It increases their level of awareness of you (if they are monitoring their own name mentions). Remember: Sharing is Caring!

A word of caution, do verify the links you retweet. You might be rickrolled (kind of a 'bait and switch'), forward spam, or worse. Good people do get hacked, so verify each and every link you pass on to your following. If done correctly, retweeting will increases your traffic and help you connect to other niche related content creators.

In the business world, it is all about the relationships we build that helps to determine our success. Retweeting is a great way to build relationships with customers, potential clients, and colleagues in the field. Retweeting gives word of mouth marketing new meaning!

> ***Tip***: If you are sending out a message that you hope gets retweeted, you actually need your entire post to be short enough to allow for @attribution. In other words, your messages should optimally be 120-122 characters. Make it easy for someone to resend your messages.

Here are some examples of retweets done well:

GOOD EXAMPLE OF A RETWEET

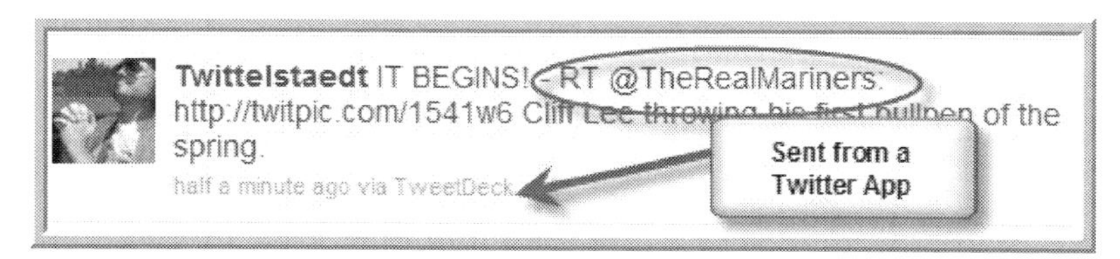

GOOD EXAMPLE OF A RETWEET

This is an excellent example of how to credit multiple posters:

EXAMPLE OF MULTIPLE RETWEET CITATION

Tracking and monitoring RT's from your PC on Twitter itself is a daunting task, but there are several web based tools you can use. Here are just a few to explore:

Retweetist: Tracks your name or a URL (link).

Retweetradar: Follows trending topics and exhibits them in a tag cloud.

Tweetmeme: Posts the most frequently retweeted messages organized by categories.

If you prefer to track retweets from your mobile phone try some of these mobile applications:

Retweet iPhone: Tracks most popular urls trending on Twitter.

Tweetmeme Mobile: Mobile version of Tweetmeme.

Tweetie: Trending tweets and search functions for RT's

Case Example: *Anthony Stevens, developer of Crowdify (http://crowdify.com/) has created a crowd sourcing application that gathers an audience in the form of respondents to a survey site. His inspiration was the highly successful social media efforts of the Barack Obama election campaign. The results provide semantic analysis that can be highly usable for brand managers, consumer relations experts, etc.*

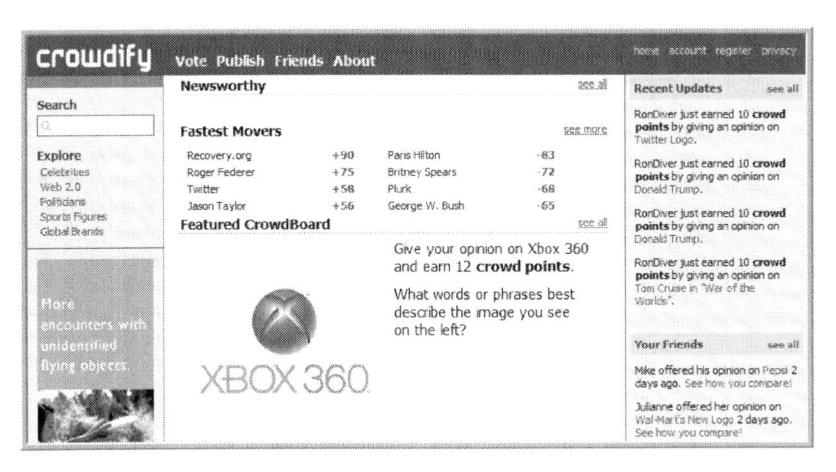

WWW.CROWDIFY.COM HOME PAGE

While the tool is still in early alpha stages, Stevens has found Twitter a terrific resource not only to find early alpha users, but also for searching for trends related to brands. Stevens also uses Twitter to both post test questions and stimulate interest in users signing up for the site both from his [*www.Twitter*](http://www.Twitter)*.com/anthonyrstevens account. He has found that the power of Twitter is not in his original tweets about Crowdify, but in his friends retweets.*

Recently @shannonevans posted a tweet about an ezine article titled: *Smart Tips for Twitter Users – How to Tweet and Not Sound Like a Twit.* To see where it had been re-published or shared beyond the first degree of contacts of @shannonevans, a quick Google Search was conducted:

GOOGLE SEARCH RESULTS

Notice the number of listings appearing in the search results beyond the first two, where www.Twitter.com/shannonevans posted the original article on two sites. The rest are either retweets or bloggers, who picked up the article and posted it.

The Tweetmeme site reported more than 17 other Tweeters had shared the article (some without the original attribute to @shannonevans):

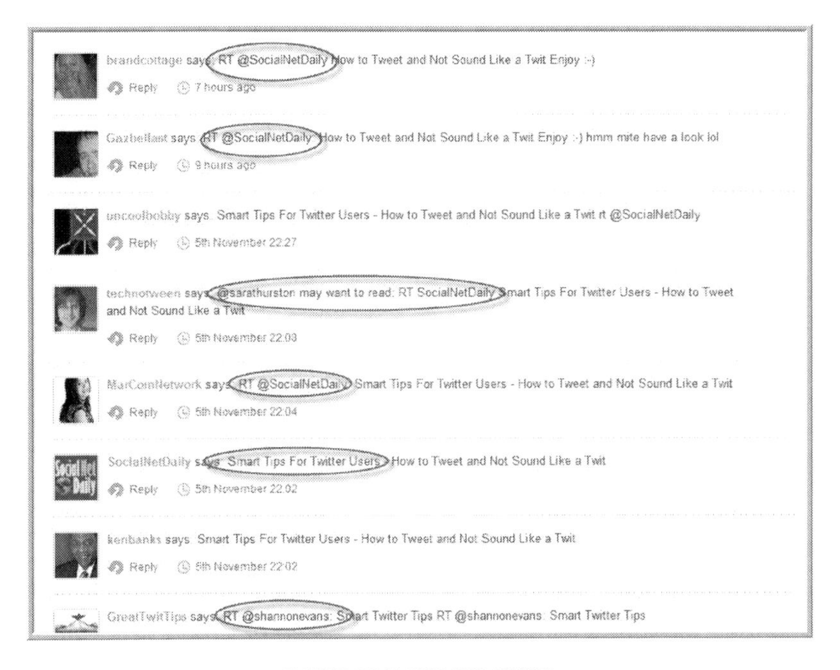

TWEETMEME SEARCH RESULTS

This opens up not only a new group of people to follow perhaps, but perhaps a great resource for dialogue with people with similar interests.

There are tons of Tweeters out there that provide no value to the Twitter stream. There are empty chatters and there are spammers. Empty chats give nothing of value.

Empty chatter: Thanks for the follow...followed by *here's my...*

Spammers act like carnies, they only huck their wares. They are not givers or influencers. They just want you to part with your money!

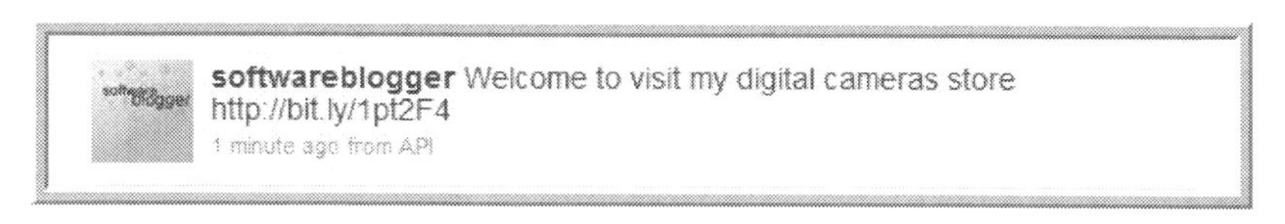

Make your content interesting, provide good links, respond to others, and ask questions that evoke more than a "yes" or "no" answer.

Retweet often! Retweeting is an important part of the Twitter experience. It is a way to share information and to foster good will with the person whose content you are sharing. Retweeting is a great way to get the attention of the original owner of the content and it fosters good will quickly in your Twitter following.

So how do I retweet? First find someone you follow whose post is probably of interest to my followers. Twitter has a retweet button after each tweet that makes it easy to retweet material to your followers. On the lower right side of each individual tweet a 'reply' and 'retweet' button appears. Select 'retweet' to share the tweet.

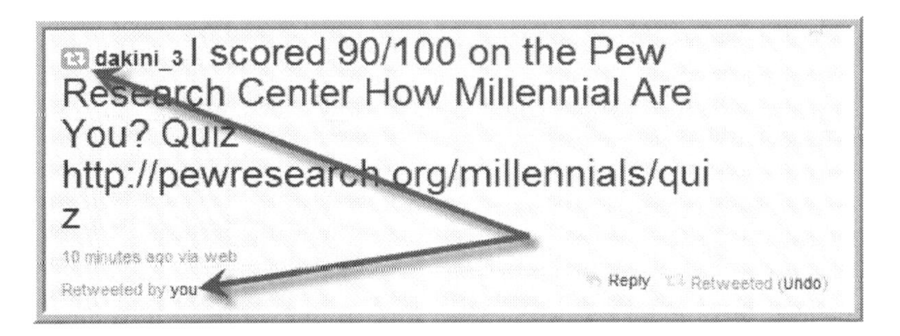

RETWEETING DIRECTLY FROM THE TWITTERSTREAM

If you are using an application like Tweetdeck or Hootsuite or a smartphone application use the RT button on the screen. It is a great way to build rapport with customers and vendors because your tweet totally benefits them. But do be careful what you RT as it implies endorsement.

This is a retweet that gives credit to the original poster. Crediting ideas and sources is always a good thing regardless of the forum. Twitter is no exception!

@HARDLYNORMAL RETWEETING @BAKESPACE'S MESSAGE

@Hardlynormal's retweet might indicate a trend. It includes a hashtag, #Halloween, and a link to a site with more information.

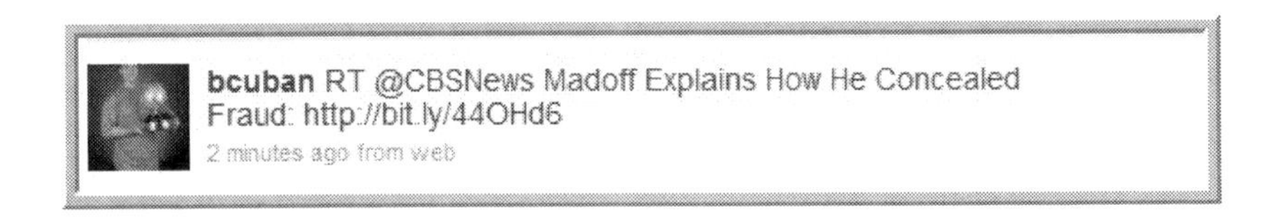

This is a straightforward retweet of a useful or important post that was timely and of high interest.

Direct Messages or DM: A direct message is a private message to someone on Twitter who is following you. They are not public as they are only seen by the author of the message and the addressed recipient. To do this directly on Twitter, you use the "message" link on the person's profile page.

You can reply to a Twitter update privately from your Twitterstream or from your phone. If someone has direct message text and email notifications "on" they will get their DM's either via email or over their phone. Keep in mind that while DM's seem like mini emails, they are not. When they are deleted by the sender, they are also deleted from the message stream of the receiver. It is possible to delete the message before the receiver even reads it! To DM someone on Twitter you use the direct message link on the right navigation panel.

You can do the same thing with your Twitter client (Hootsuite, TweetDeck, etc) on your computer or from your phone's Twitter application. If the person is following you, simply follow this format in the "What are you doing" dialogue box:

D (*person's name*) message you want to send.

You can also send a direct message from the reply message within your direct message 'inbox'. From your home page go to the right hand side of the page and select "Direct Messages:"

SELECT DIRECT MESSAGE TO SEND A PRIVATE NOTE

You can now leave a direct message to that person.

DIRECT MESSAGE 'WINDOW'

You can direct message by using the reply to a regular Tweet from the person. Click the arrow at the end of the update and you will see "@username" in the update screen. Simply remove the "@" symbol and replace it with a letter "d" and a space. Then type a message.

Tips: DM's are abused and are ignored in many instances by recipients. Keep in mind when DMing:

- Don't DM to tell the person you are following them or to “thank you and here's a free gift/ebook/etc.“
- Don't DM to tell them you are following them, but they are not following you.
- Don't DM to welcome someone and then ask them to visit your blog or website.
- Don't @username to send a one on one answer to others. It is clutters the Twitterstream and isn't a chat room!
- Don't DM to post your follower count or ask people to recruit others to follow you. That is really tacky!
- Don't DM them and tell them you just added them to your Mafia Family
- DM”s should provide value, relate to the follower's interests, be transparent, and respectful.
- Do DM to tell someone you found their post or blog especially useful or interesting.
- Do DM to thank someone for retweeting an especially important message.
- Do DM when you need to send personal or non-public messages.

Hashtags: What are hashtags and how do you use them? On Twitter, there are often words preceded by the # hash symbol. These hashtag prefixes make it easy for people to search for tweets based on a common theme: #olympics or #redsox.

HASHTAGS FOR THE 2010 OLYMPICS

Hastags (#word) let you track topics, posts, events, etc in an indexable and searchable format. Adding a hashtag lets you aggregate a whole series of related conversations. Use hashtags to have a discussion in a particular audience setting or to stimulate conversation. It is also a great way to have a discussion with a particular audience listening in on a particular event.

For example, if you search #smbseattle, you will get tweets that are about Social Media Breakfast Seattle and their events or discussions. You will not pick up Server Message Blocks in Seattle or Small and Medium Businesses Seattle. You will only get a list of tweets related to Social Media Breakfast Seattle because someone has marked it as a specific topic to find and share:

HASHTAG VARIATIONS FOR SOCIAL MEDIA BREAKFAST SEATTLE

Hastags are also how tweeters add additional metadata (a message that tells search engines about the data so it can be searched) to tweets to make them "tagged" and easier to follow and search. Create a hashtag just by placing hastag symbol (#) in front of a word or abbreviation. For example:

In order for users to create groupings on Twitter, hashtags were instituted. If they remind you of DOS (then you also remember rotary phones), you are right. They allow real-time tracking of conversations and specific subjects.

So where do hashtags come from? Do you ask for one from Twitter or can you create your own? Twitter is about the immediacy of the moment and real time information at your fingertips. In that vein, anyone can create a hashtag just by adding it to a tweet.

When the youth of Iran began to march in the streets in protest to the election tampering there, some Twitter user wrote a post and added #iran and #iranelection. It is not really clear who posted first, but it was read by someone else, who posted it in their tweet or retweeted about the protests and the savage retaliation by the government. It took on a life of its own.

The same thing happened when a plane safely ditched in the Hudson River. Whoever posted the hashtag #flight1549 for the crash landing in the river scooped all the news networks. That simple hashtag went viral immediately!

It does not matter where the hashtag falls in the message. It can be at the beginning, middle or end and it is still searchable, cataloged, and easy for users to find. It is just a great way for Twitter users to sort through the unrelated messages and get to the one they are trying to follow.

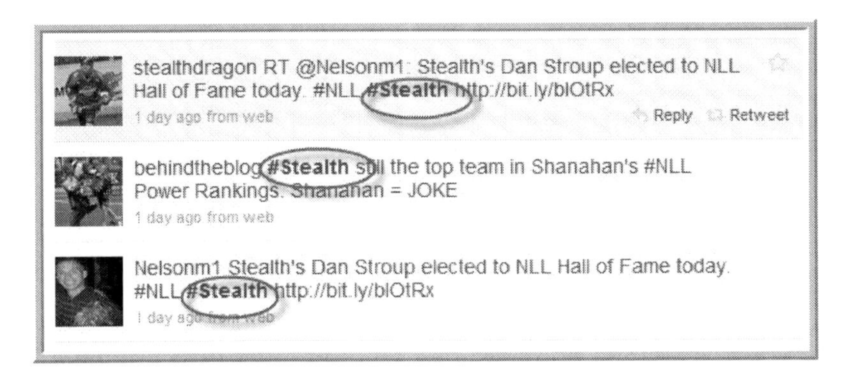

Hashtags create an easy way to track a subject for further reference. With this said, it is important to consider the proliferation of hashtags used by spammers. Spammers use a hashtag attached to a totally unrelated tweet.

Event planners and conference organizers often promote their hashtag so all the tweets are grouped for coordinating meet-ups, schedule changes, etc. So if you want to create a hashtag you want to use something that captures the idea or topic to be followed, but that is also brief enough not to eat up too many of your 140 characters. You also want to do a brief Twitter search on the tag you select to see if there are other shorter variations in existence (that is a good thing usually!). When a hashtag is used at an event, you can follow a conversation regardless of whether you are following the person who posted the tweets with the hashtag.

How do you effectively disseminate information on Twitter with hashtags? Depending on your purpose and plan for your company's use of Twitter as a broadcast mechanism, you can use hashtags a multitude of ways.

If you are a community bookstore, you probably would not want to use the #lusciousladies hashtag for the much heralded launch of a book on MGM Studio's women of the golden era. You might want to label it #greatreads or #Glamoryears. If you are a local brewery, you might want to use #thirstythursdays to tweet about your specials or a special event.

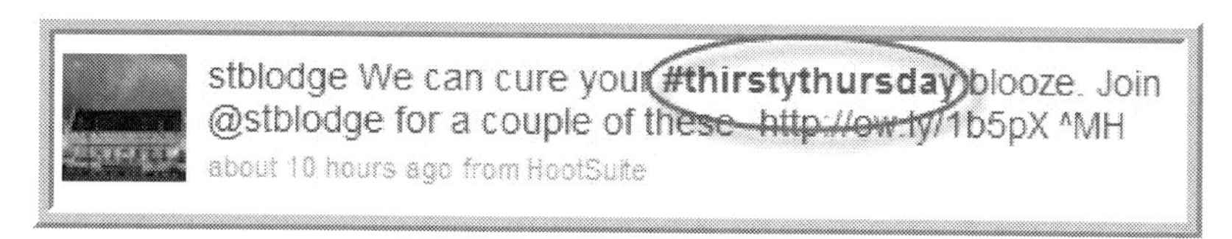

#THIRSTYTHURSDAY

To explore some hashtags, you can go to a few searchable directories that catalog hashtags and are fairly easy to use. Use hashtags to create topics that others can use and search. Use keywords when creating a hashtag. Some useful Hashtag applications to cxplore:

Tweetmapper: Use hashtags to map your location

TweetChat: Tracking hashtags in real-time

Hash-Dump: Use to register a new hashtags for credit

What the Trend: www.whatthetrend.com more of a user based wiki it explains hashtags and even investigates which trends are spam filled and includes a brief description of the associated material to the hashtag.

Hashtags.org: provides details about the hashtag's contents and the frequency of occurrence on Twitter.

Twubs: a directory that aggragates hashtags based on categories and trends.

Delve into Twitter and see what others in your industry are talking about that is on topic and in alignment with your organization. If you see something that is of interest to your followers and is right for your business, then create tweets using those hashtags or go create one.

It is important to realize that businesses can use hashtags as tactical tools to track social media campaigns and to build your social business presence with potential and existing customers. Create a memorable hashtag that works for your business strategically and supports audience engagement.

The San Diego fires of 2007 were hashtagged by Nate Ritter as #sandiegofire. He used this to identify his fire related tweets. Since those fires and his tweets they have taken on a life of their own with Twitter users. They are used at events, conferences, contests, recall notices, webinars, disasters, quotes, product launches and conversations.

If you are hosting/attending an event or doing a presentation, Twitter provides a real time method to connect those who are "there" with those who are in attendance, as well as those who are not. Create a unique hashtag for the event and encourage those present or watching via "livestream" to post during the presentation. It is a great way to share experiences as they unfold and to push out key talking points for a more global perspective! Not only is this a new method for communicating, but it actually can enhance the total experience of the event. What a cool way to have your clients and customers interact and experience an event!

Use Hashtags to:

Follow:

- key topics
- new products
- brand mentions

Create:

- links
- interesting content
- responses to others

There are no real rules for the use of hashtags. They are useful for tracing and tracking conversations. Use them sparingly and when they add value to the conversation. If you use them in every tweet, you will confuse, frustrate, or anger your followers.

Be authentic, be brief, and be transparent and your followers will come back for more! When the CEO/owner of a company interacts with their community, a positive rapport begins that creates a strong presence.

Hashtags are just a good way to share information on specific topics with your followers. They are really useful for pre-announcing or issuing invitations to a webinar or live site presentation. If you are using slides you can use the hashtag on the first slide and remind participants that you have a hashtag for the event. Let's say you are attending a sales related event hosted by @nialldevitt. You could create a related hashtag - #topsalesexperts – and send out tweets mentioning the presenters' names:

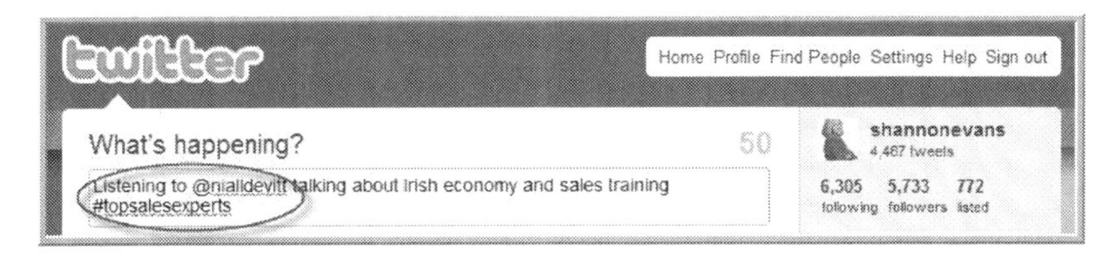

This use of a hashtag allows for discussion online that is easy to follow or track by the participants as well as those who can't attend, yet can "listen" via Twitter on their phone or computer. It gets people who are present to share your message with their followers. Often, you will see a spike in online attendance half way through your presentation because people hear about it or see your event trending on Twitter. Hashtags are great for crowd sourcing and creating a buzz around your event, and even better, it lets those in attendance to become your viral marketer to *their* followers.

If you want to make your events interactive, you can engage those who are participating through Twitter by fielding questions associated with the hashtag. It is as if you are saying "I hear you and want to know your problems." This is taking the 'one of us' presentation styles to questions and you help to resolve their questions. When listeners feel that they are part of the event they have more "buy in" and the Twitter followers online are motivated to check your website for more detailed information.

The Washington State Wine Association of growers and vintners hosts a Twitter event to promote their merlots as #WaMerlot, and tastings are held around the state. Many of the participants hold virtual conversations around that hashtag not only around the state of Washington, but hashtagged comments are added by vintners and wine connoisseurs around the globe!

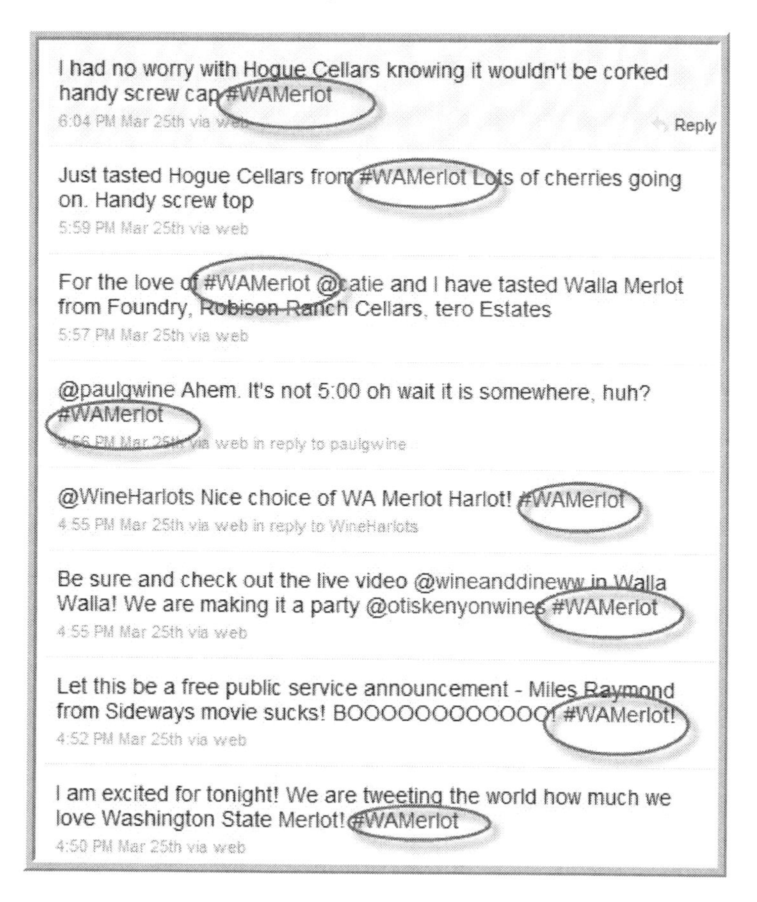

WASHINGTON MERLOT #WAMERLOT HASHTAG

A really easy way to initiate viral campaigns for your followers is to create a hashtag that promotes specials, awareness, or recognizes a new employee. One service provider makes numbered hashtags with keywords and tells their followers on their site to mention the hashtag by number to get a discount on special services. This way they know how people hear about them on Twitter! Create a

#followfriday type of hashtag so your followers can comment, provide feedback, and promote for you.

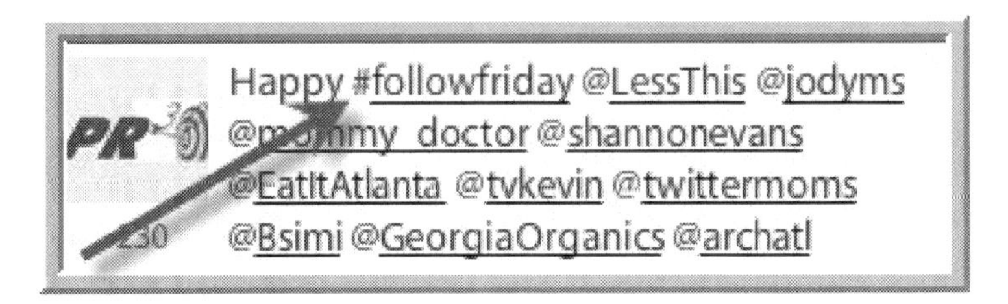

In between broadcasts about your discounts and specials, become a source of community news. Talk about things that impact your clients. Promote other local businesses. Post about issues that affect your clients and that are related to your industry. Be that "go to" recognized website for good, useful, information that your customer base relates to and wants to read.

To implement a hashtag, you will first want to see if the one you wish to use is already in use. Search for it in the Twitter search field. If it is not in use, create one that is short, recognizable and easy to remember. Place the "#" sign in front of any alpha-numeric combination. Then tell others about it. Let's say that you are attending the World Gadget Tradeshow and you want to see if others are talking about it on Twitter.

Go to www.search.Twitter.com and lookup #wgt and #worldgadgettradeshow. If not used, create the shortest version. If the same hashtag you want to use is in use and it is the same tradeshow, see who is talking and perhaps join in the discussions.

Case Example: *Freelance writing professional Lydia Dishman, known on Twitter as LydiaBreakfast, participated in a hashtagged conversation labeled #journchat. She wanted to talk about the business of freelancing in an informal forum with other writers. She and the others involved wanted an informal forum for networking, discussing ideas, and to just talk about the business involved with free lancing. Thus was created #editorchat, which Lydia and Tim Beyers co-moderate every Wednesday night with a list of three to four questions and a cast of various voyeurs, participants.*

@milehighfool #editorchat My 1st freelance assignment came from seeing a tweet about a market guide being open for queries.

quirkywriter, [+] Fri 12 Mar 19:38 via TweetDeck

#Writer tweeps: reply if you have stories about getting more assignments/business from Twitter. #editorchat

milehighfool, [+] Fri 12 Mar 19:28 via Chromed Bird

@karimacatherine #journchat #blogchat #editorchat and people I happen to see who live near me

KakieF, [+] Tue 09 Mar 17:54 via web

Post on my blog "To PLR or Not" at http://tinyurl.com/y8qgl2p, #freelance, #editorchat, #copywriter, #smallBizChat, #writechat

RJ_Medak, [+] Tue 09 Mar 15:46 via TweetDeck

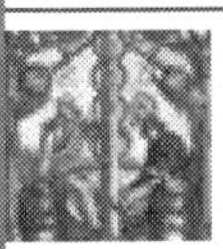

Barnes & Noble to Bundle Print and eBooks - make content available across multiple screens and devices http://bit.ly/9tIKrJ #editorchat

Dark_Faust, [+] Mon 08 Mar 09:40 via TweetDeck

#EDITORCHAT SEARCH RESULTS

There are guest editors, authors, and publishers who discuss the business of writing. According to www.Twitter.com/lydiabreakfast, she and Tim (www.Twitter.com/milehighfool) have developed relations with many writers they would not have otherwise met. While they have had to move the actual forum to a more robust platform that supports their rapid fire discussions and large audience, it all started on Twitter and is still heavily promoted there.

URL's: Adding URL's to your Tweets has to be done judiciously, so as not to appear to be a spamming huckster. Post links to your latest blog entry with a direct link to the page where the latest entry resides. Do this carefully. Lead in with a great headline. Don't be one of those who say, "See my latest blog post – www.itsallaboutme.com". This is considered rather obnoxious behavior.

Good Examples:

Bad Example:

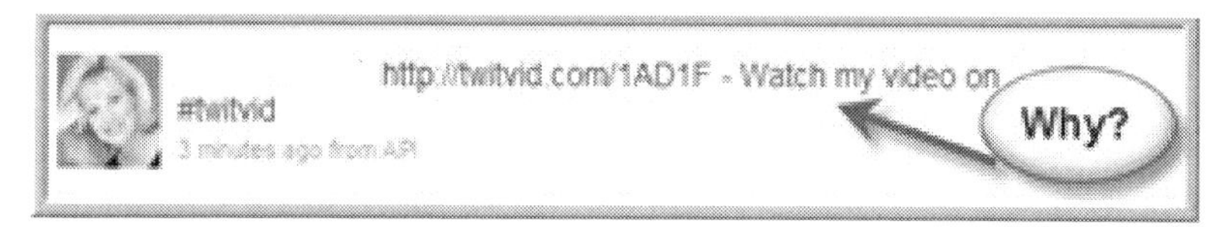

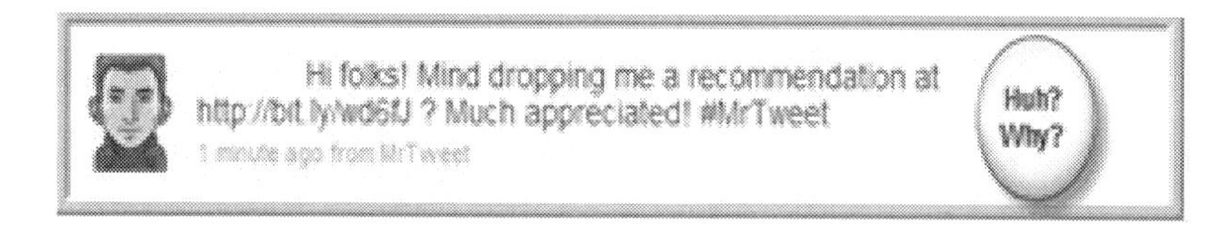

Blog and article URLs tend to be lengthy and eat up much of the 140 character limit of a single Twitter message. Tiny URLs are used to shorten links to your blog, a great resource, or a good article on the web. Using commercial URL shortening vendors like Hootsuite, Bit.ly and BudUrl allows you to not only abbreviate or customize links, but also to track the click-thru's to the link. The resulting analytics are incredibly informative for letting you know what was useful and valuable to your followers.

Brand promotion is acceptable on Twitter if you do not over-promote and do it with class. You may be perceived as a spammer with excessive self-promotional updates. Sparse links to your blog are permissible if you make it interesting to your following. Try and be uniquely useful!

Here are some really specific examples of Twitter spam messages that will get you unfollowed really quickly:

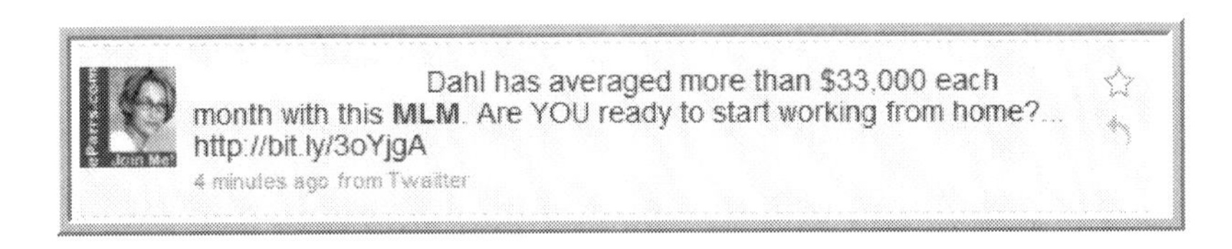

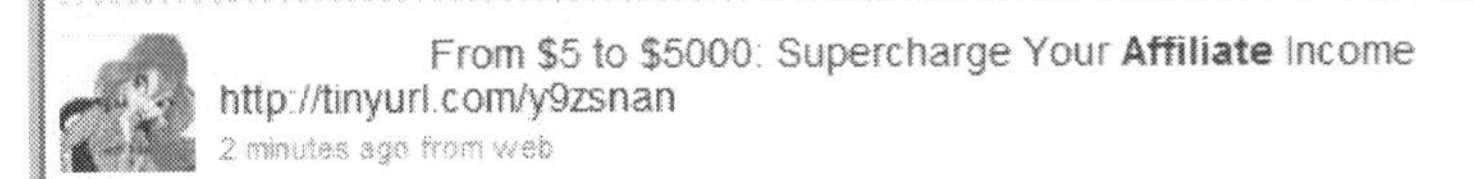

Most people will block and delete you without ever giving you a reason if you post material like this. There are some people who just never "get it" and always wonder why they can't build a viable following on Twitter.

There are also the blog announcers. They tell you they have a new blog post, but you have no clue what the topic is and if you dare go read it for fear of getting spammed or picking up a dreaded computer virus:

It is far better to give your readers at least an interesting lead in to decide if they want to go read your latest blog entry. Give them a hint to the content:

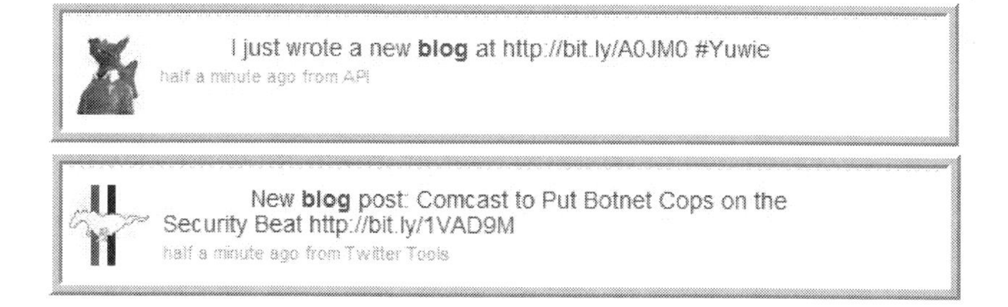

TweetingRules:

Once you understand the basic principles and processes of Tweeting rules, you are ready to actually use Twitter to leverage its potential. The following is merely a starting point for how to actively participate effectively:

Frequency: How often should you tweet? Can you over-tweet? Tweeting is a fine balance between talking and listening. Some people will unfollow you if you tweet (no matter how useful the content) too often. Then again, some people will unfollow you if you don't tweet often enough!

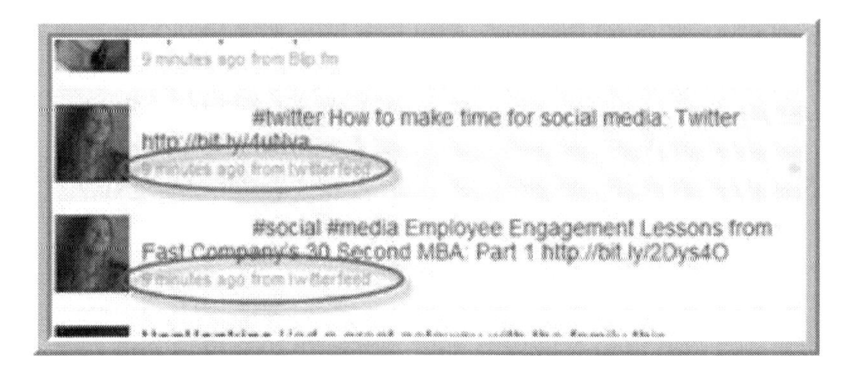

MULTIPLE TWEETS SENT SIMULTANEOUSLY

A good rule of thumb is to listen, share, listen, interact, converse, give, and then listen some more. Just don't ramble about your kids, your in-laws, your coffee/alcohol consumption, or your toileting habits. Mindless "Twibble" is not useful and will get you quickly unfollowed!

Under-tweeting is just as bad as over-tweeting. It can result in some people culling you from those they follow. Some people use Twitter clients that among other things, allow you to schedule previously crafted tweets for later delivery. If you don't have time to Tweet at least once per day you need to use a dashboard like Hootsuite that lets you schedule tweets ahead of time. You could set up tweets that are based around great articles you find during the week which you then parcel out using your scheduling feature of your dashboard application. Set aside time on your work calendar to set up a week's worth of Tweets.

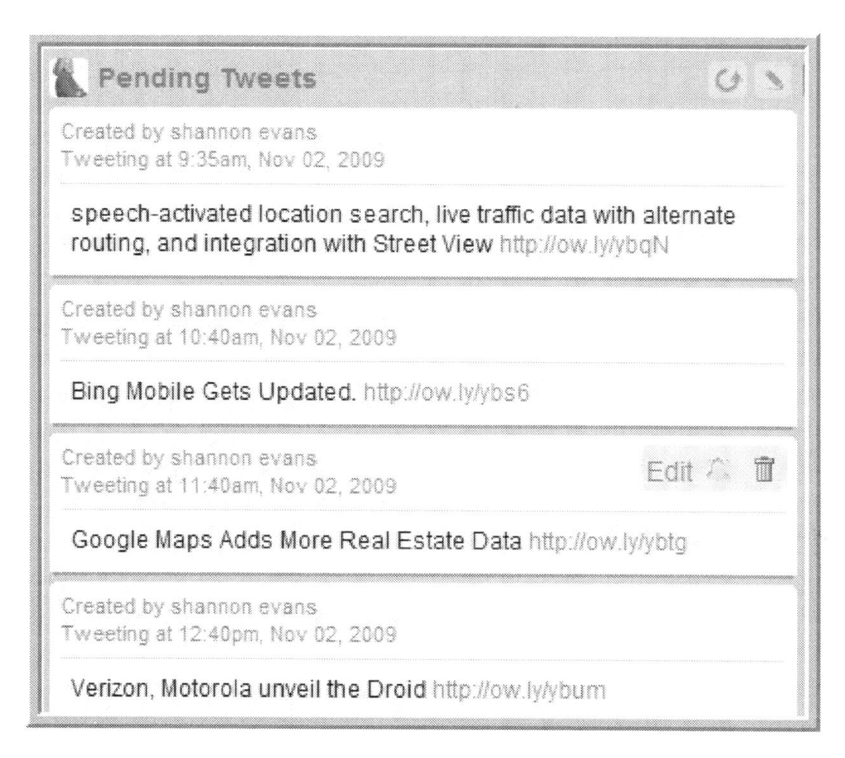

HOOTSUITE DASHBOARD TWEET VIEW

Regardless of how often you tweet or how you tweet, you still have to make the time to engage with those around you. You must also monitor for brand mentions, important discussions, etc. It only takes a few minutes a day and the pay off can have great significance for your brand.

Check your replies often (at least once per day) to see what other people are saying about you or your brand. Click on your @yourname on the right side of your Twitter page to check your messages. Followers will reach out to you with the @yourname to ask you questions, answer questions you asked, and often to comment about your tweets, Responding to others not only builds rapport andgets the attention of your followers, it also attracts new followers.

How to Rapidly Increase Your Following on Twitter

One of the best ways to get your Twitter profile out and in front of your clients and customers is to add a link to your email signature.

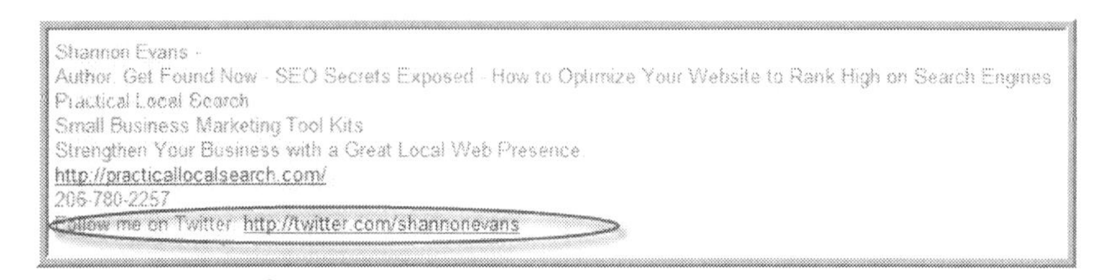

EMAIL SIGNATURE WITH TWITTER LINK

Add it to your other social media profiles like Facebook and LinkedIn:

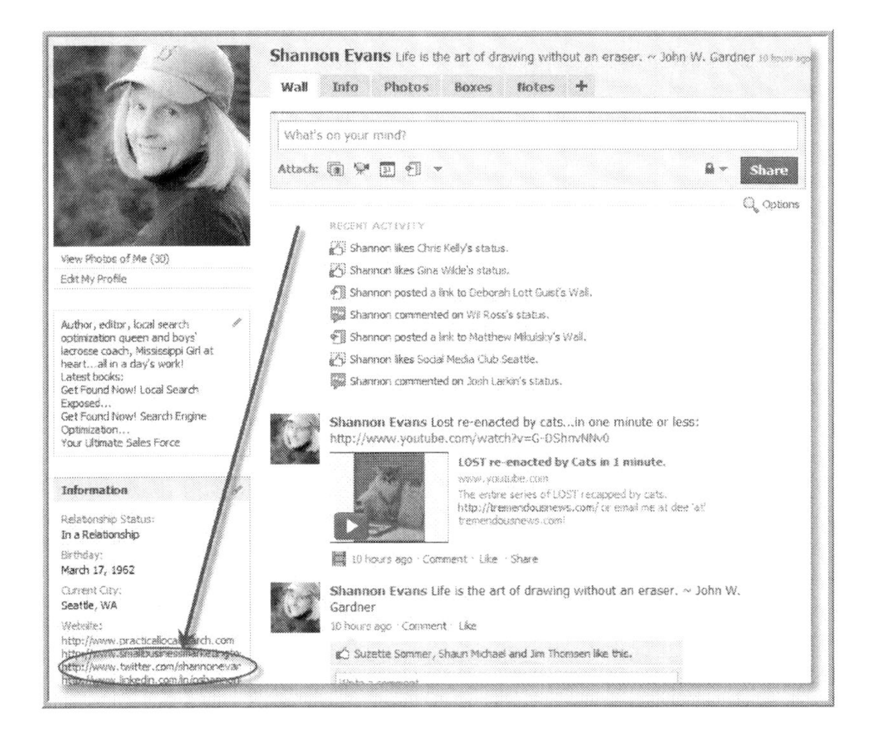

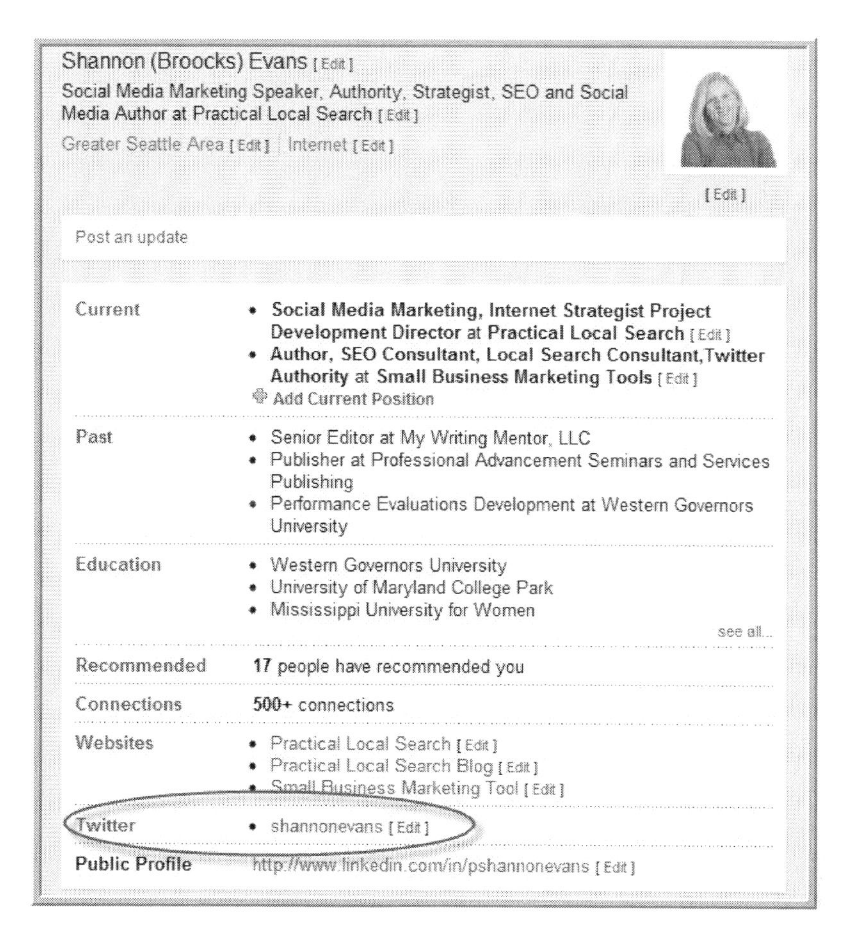

TWITTER LINK ON LINKEDIN PROFILE

Use it with social bookmarking tools like Digg and Stumbleupon. These are all critical elements to get more exposure for your marketing efforts and to develop a dedicated following.

Get additional targeted followers by adding your Twitter account to some categories in various directories:

Twello: Categorized directory of public Twitter accounts. http://www.twellow.com/

Just Tweet It: Twitter directory organized by genre http://justtweetit.com/directory/

We Follow: Twitter directory organized by categories based on user-selected personal areas of interests http://wefollow.com/

Loaded Web: Geo-targeted directory of blogs, businesses, and Twitter accounts http://www.loadedweb.com/Twitter/

Tweet Find: Directory of Twittering Businesses and Users http://www.tweetfind.com/

Tweeplepages: Directory of Twitter users organized by user interests, keywords, as well as areas of expertise http://tweeplepages.com/

After you list your Twitter profile, go back on those directories and follow people in your niche. When you follow people, they are more likely to follow you back.

Case Example: *Mike O'Neil, author of "Rock the World with Your Online Presence" and a professional presenter, uses Twitter to help promote his LinkedIn.com "rock star" persona. He has used Twitter to promote his book with contests and links with great success.*

Mike is also a Twitter tool junkie, and Hootsuite is his tool of choice. With Hootsuite Mike is able to manage his two accounts' tweets all in one program: (www.Twitter.com/IASocialMedia) and www.Twitter.com/MikeONeilDenver).

MIKE O'NEIL PERSONAL TWITTER ACCOUNT

MIKE O'NEIL'S PROFESSIONAL BUSINESS NAME TWITTER ACCOUNT

He uses targeted keywords on directory sites like Twellow to find others accounts to follow, who use words like "CEO", "Leader", "Author", and "Rockstar" in their profile. As Mike was gearing up for the pre-launch of his book, he used Twitter to drive followers to participate in a contest for "Best LinkedIn Profile". He posted both his Twitter 'handle' (user name) and his LinkedIn public profile to create a buzz about the contest. For those who are tempted to post their Twitter updates on LinkedIn Mike has these words of caution, "Automated Twitter updates on LinkedIn are a real No-No. LinkedIn is a place for project updates and not status updates!"

Chapter 7: Tweet From Your Mobile Device

Twitter is a great tool for reaching mobile phone users. In the U.S., you can send text messages to mobile phones without requiring their phone number. This is important because if they perceive they are receiving spam from senders, they can turn off specific notifications or even unfollow the sender. Try doing that from a land line!

To have access to your Twitter account from your mobile phone, you will need to go to Twitter.com and log in to your Twitter account. Once there select the "Settings" tab from the top of your home page.

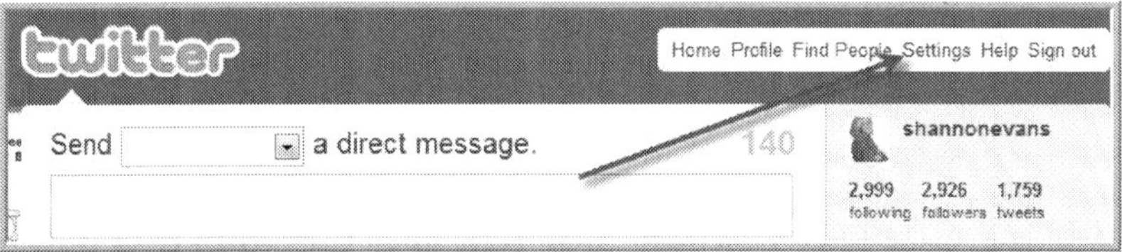

SELECT "SETTINGS"

A new page will open. Select the "Devices" tab at the top of the page.

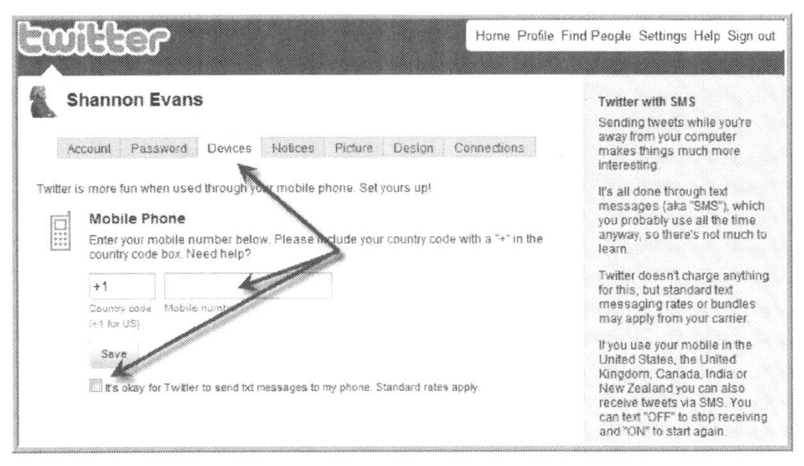

Input your complete cell phone number in the text box and select "save" to receive Twitter updates on your cell phone. Select "ok" at the bottom of the page to enable sending text messages from Twitter to your phone. Twitter will send you a message confirming the link. You can now update your Twitter status and receive messages from your cell phone.

When you want to stop Twitter updates sent to your phone, text the word "off" to 40404 or go to the Twitter web site to stop them. Some mobile Twitter clients let you set your updates to "sleep" during scheduled hours so you are not disturbed at work, temple, church, or at the doctor's office.

Some SMS/Cell Phone Twitter Clients:

Mobiscape: Twitter client for BlackBerry phones http://www.getapp.in/mobiscape/

Dabr: Open source Mobile Web aApp for Twitter for S60, Android, the iPhone and Blackberry http://dabr.co.uk/

Tweete: Features user timelines, replies, direct messages, users, favorites. http://m.tweete.net/login

Skyfire: Mobile browser that supports flash for Windows Mobile and Symbian devices. http://www.skyfire.com/

TweetNGo: Twitter client for the iPhone and iPod Touch.

TweetTime: Supports multiple accounts, uploading pictures from camera and library. You get it at the app store http://www.appstorehq.com/tweettime-iphone-62974/app

Simple Tweet: iPhone application to post, remove and add friends from your iPhone. http://itunes.apple.com/WebObjects/MZStore.woa/wa/viewSoftware?id=309261180&mt=8

Twitterlerts: Twitter client with Search and Alerts
http://www.appsafari.com/utilities/4635/Twitter-alerts/

TweetCaster: Twitter app for BlackBerry can manage multiple Twitter accounts. Free in exchange for one tweet
http://www.handmark.com/company/apps/tweetcaster/blackberry.php

Openbreak: Mobile client for posting updates to Twitter.
http://www.orangatame.com/products/openbeak/

Twibble: Mobile client for Java enabled devices (Nokia, Blackberry. http://www.twibble.de/twibble-mobile/

According to Denise Barnes, author of *How F.U.N.K.Y. is Your Cell Phone*, "technology continues to evolve at such an accelerating rate, many professionals are now become mobilized. There are mobile SEO tools and Social Networking Applications that can be used to empower mobile professionals who desire to take the convenience of the office on the go…"

You can find tools that are specific to your device, Wireless Application Protocol (WAP) based Apps, or Text based (SMS) services to use Social Networking services especially for Twitter. The following pages contain some of the many options for using Twitter while sitting at the airport, in a taxicab, or even at the gym.

Device Specific Apps:

iPhone:

Pinger	Tweetmeme	Gypsii Chorus
TweetOut	Tweetie	Jott
iTweet2	ThinCloud	Advark Twizzle
RocketVox	TweetSwitch	Netlog LogPost
Twalk.in		Hootsuite
Twitter 3D		TweetDeck
MobileTwitterrific		MobyPicture
TweetPocket		Netlog
Fring		Just Update
Twittelator		PocketTweets

Android:

TwitterDroid	Twidroid	RocketVox
Netlog	LogPost	Seesmic
MobyPicture	TwitterRide	Swift

Blackberry:

Gypsii	Twitterberry	Jott
Loopt	GetMobio	Blackbird
Twitter2Go	RocketVox	LogPost
UberTwitter	Seesmic	Twibble

Palm:

MoTwit	LogPost	Twitter2Go

Windows Mobile:

Tiny Twitter	Twikini	GPS Twit
LogPost	Quakk	Twitter2Go
SQIJ	PocketTwit	GetMobio
Locify	TwitToday	Twobile
Twit	RocketVox	

Nokia:		
Gypsii	Jargong	MobyPicture
Twibble	JTwitter	

WAP:

Twitter's Mobile Website: http://m.Twitter.com/login

ZAGAT.mobi: for travelers who would like to find a tweet about a specific restaurant.

Visual Twitter: Anyone can use Visual Twitter. All that's needed to use Visual Twitter is a camera phone. Simply take a picture, and send it to: me@visualTwitter.com

Twitter2Go: http://Twitter2go.com

Twitpic: http://twitpic.com/slcya

Twittme.mobi: web based Twitter application built for mobile users. http://www.twittme.mobi/

FilttrMobile: interface that helps you tweet easily- http://m.filttr.com/login.php?msg=You%20Need%20To%20

uTweetMe - http://utweetme.navetke.ru/

Twitstat: http://twit2d.com/

Slandr: a mobile site for Twitter users. You can login with your Twitter credentials and start Twittering on any mobile device: http://m.slandr.net/login.php?return=/index.php

Tweete: http://m.tweete.net/login

Twitteresce: http://code.madpilot.com.au/index.html. Note. Must have a Java enabled device.

TwitterFone: Use your mobile cell phone to update your Twitter status. http://www.Twitterfone.com

Abiro Jitter: http://www.abiro.com/lab/j2me_jitter.php.

Twitsay: Listen to voice messages on your Twitter page using this. http://twitsay.com

Topsy: This is a very cool search engine powered by Twitter. http://topsy.com

SMS (Text Based Services)

Regroup: leverages the power of email, forums, wiki, SMS, Facebook, Twitter, and more. It integrates with Twitter and Facebook and can be used to send SMS messages to your designated groups/lists http://www.regroup.com/welcome

TwitterPeek: A service that is always "on," receives direct message tweets, and allows you to view links in plain text, as well as incorporate Twitpic images.
http://www.Twitterpeek.com

Twitter Answers: Tweet questions and get answers directly. Note. You will have to create your settings in Twitter (http://Twitter.com/devices) to do this.
http://ask.mosio.com/Twitter

No matter where you go and what you want to do with mobile connecting on Twitter or any other social platform…you can bet there is an app for it!

Chapter 8: Lists - Twitter's Organization Tool

Twitter created a new feature in 2009 that allowed users to organize the people they follow in self-selected logical categorized groups. These groups allow the user to filter conversations they monitor at any given time for any given group.

Lists can be established to group people by profession, location, common interests, etc. Lists can include people you are currently following or are NOT following. This is especially useful when you want to watch certain people to see if you are interested in following them. It is also a useful feature when you hit temporary ceilings for the number of people you can follow.

Creating a Twitter List is really simple to do. First, log into your Twitter account, on your home page in the side navigation bar on the right is "Lists". Select "New List" to get started creating a customized list.

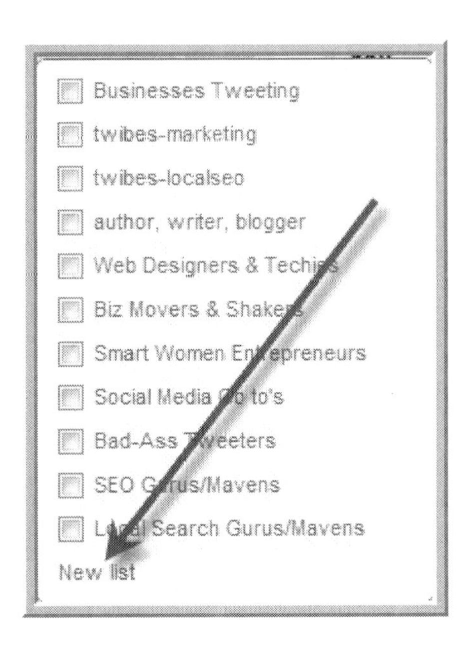

SELECT "NEW LIST"

You will then be asked to create a name for your list:

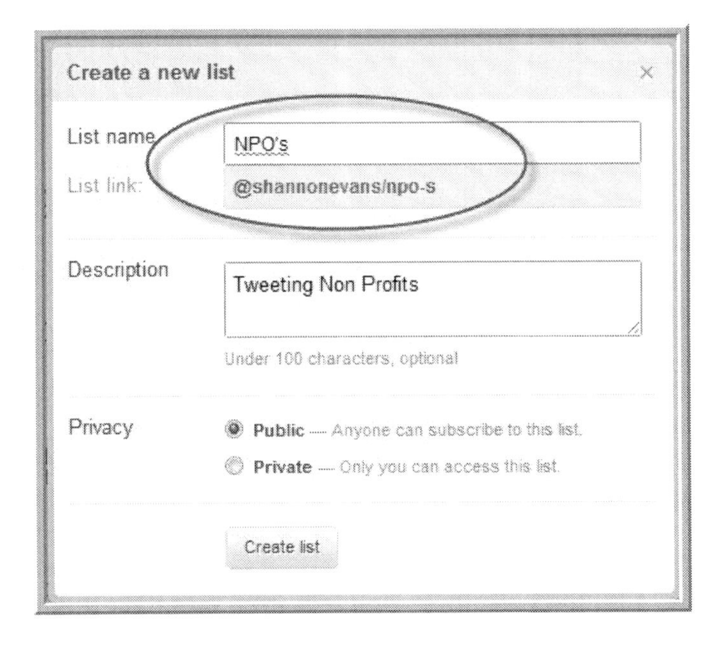

That name will become the URL for the list. For example:

"Twitter.com/shannonevans/npo-s"

You will then have two options for the new list:

Public List

Private List

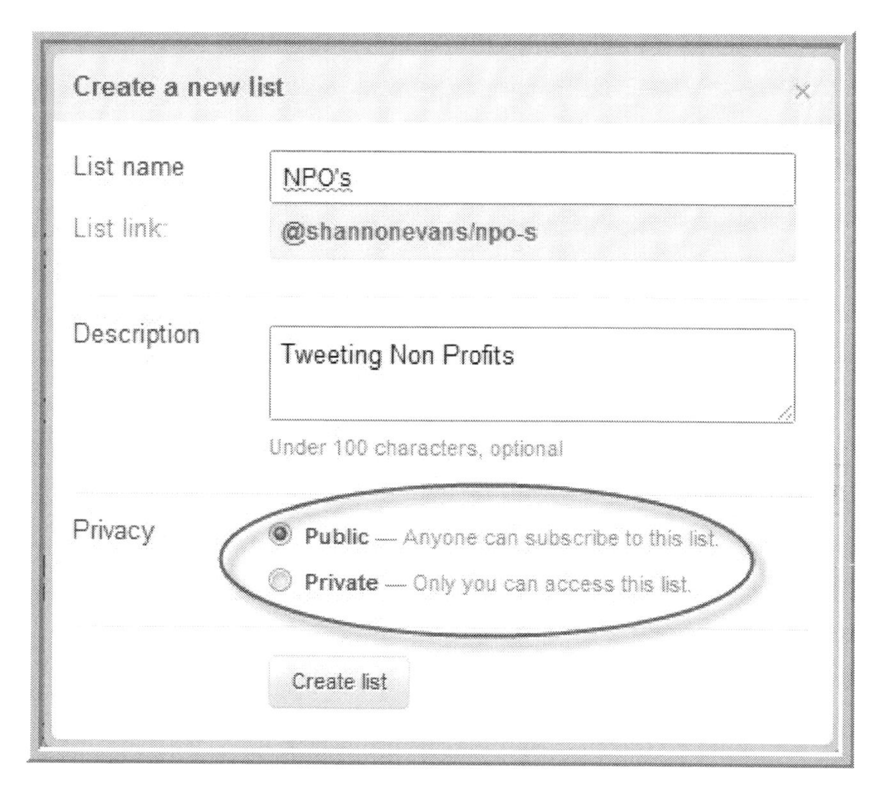

CONTROL THE ACCESSIBILITY TO YOUR LIST

Public lists are available for anyone to see or follow. Use these public lists when you want to promote or recommend some of your own followers or following. You can use it as a way to create recognition for those you might be courting for business or who you might want to attract to your community of followers.

Private lists means *only* you can see the contents of the list. The people on the list cannot even see that they are on the list. Private lists are great for monitoring your competitors or the 'negative nellies' in the Twitter stream or to just be a voycur to certain conversations.

Once you have selected 'public' or 'private' select "Create List."

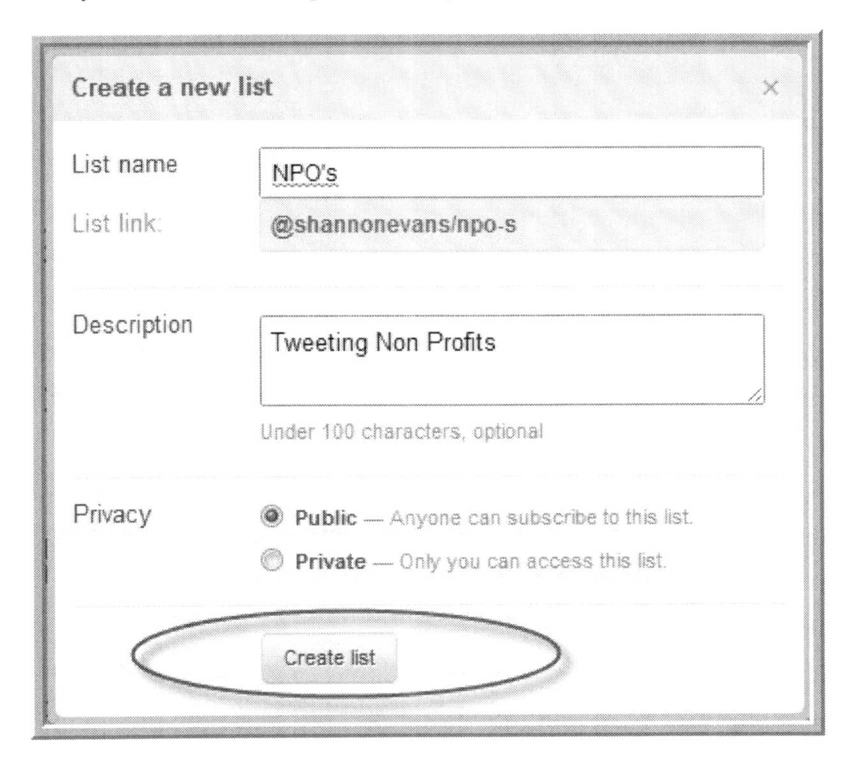

TO CREATE A NEW LIST SELECT "CREATE LIST"

Now you can start adding people to your list. There are two methods for adding people to lists: from their profile page or from any "Followers" or "Following" links on any profile page (yours or someone else's).

From Individual Profile Pages:

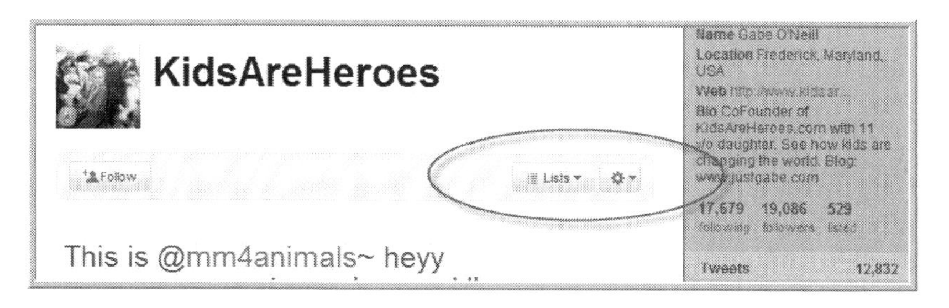

SELECT THE LISTS DROP DOWN LINK ON A USERS PROFILE PAGE

Select the 'lists' button and your menu of lists will open. Add the new individual to any of your lists with a simple click on the box to the left of the pop up list of categories:

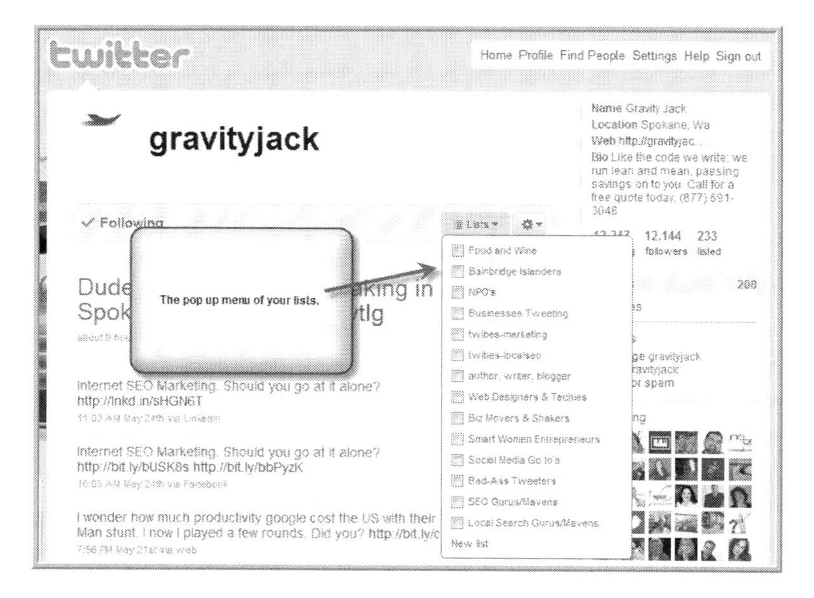

ALL YOUR LISTS WILL APPEAR TO ADD A PROFILE

From Any Followers or Following Page:

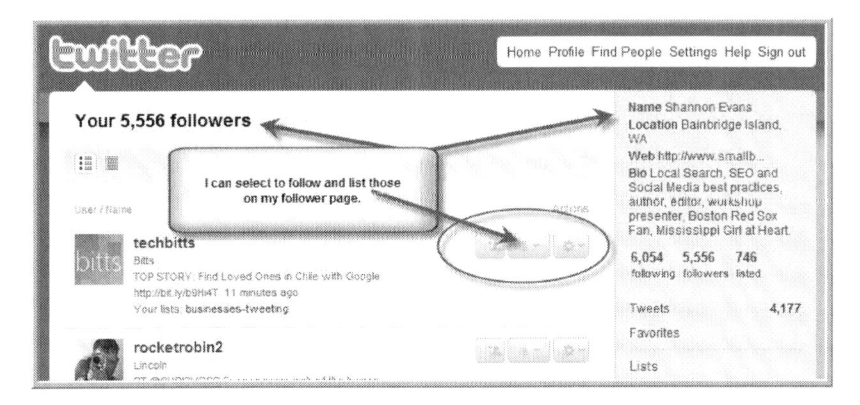

ORGANIZE FOLLOWERS WITH LISTS

Simply select the list button to the right of your follow/follower, your lists will open and you can add them to already created lists or you can create another new list:

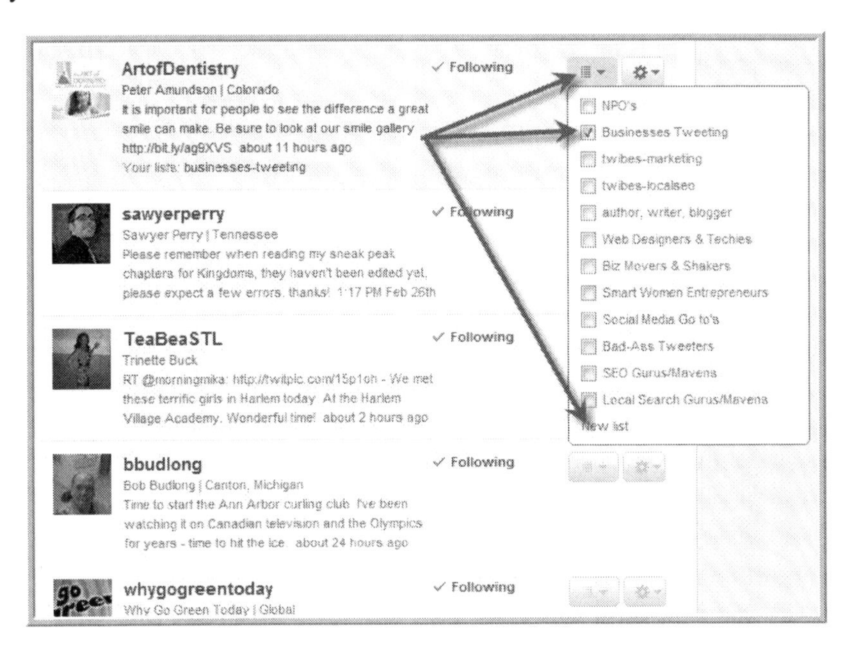

ADD FOLLOWERS FROM FOLLOWER PAGE TO YOUR LISTS

Twitter currently limits listings to 500 user names per list and a maximum of 20 total lists. There are no limits at this time to the number of lists to which *you* can be added.

NUMBER OF LISTS @MAYHEMSTUDIOS APPEARS ON

After you follow or create lists, the URLs for those lists will begin to populate the "Lists" section on the right side navigation panel of your Twitter home page..

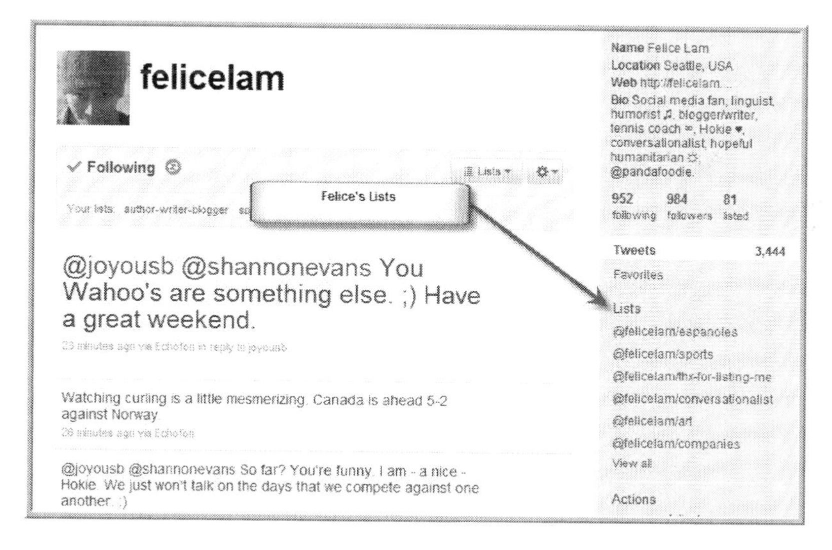

SOME OF THE LISTS @FELICELAM HAS CREATED

Once on the "home" page of www.Twitter.com/felicelam you can find that she has included you on her list you can follow the list itself without having to follow each person on the list individually. You can also see what those on the list are tweeting and determine if you want to follow the whole list itself. Or click over to learn more about them and decide if you wish to follow them individually.

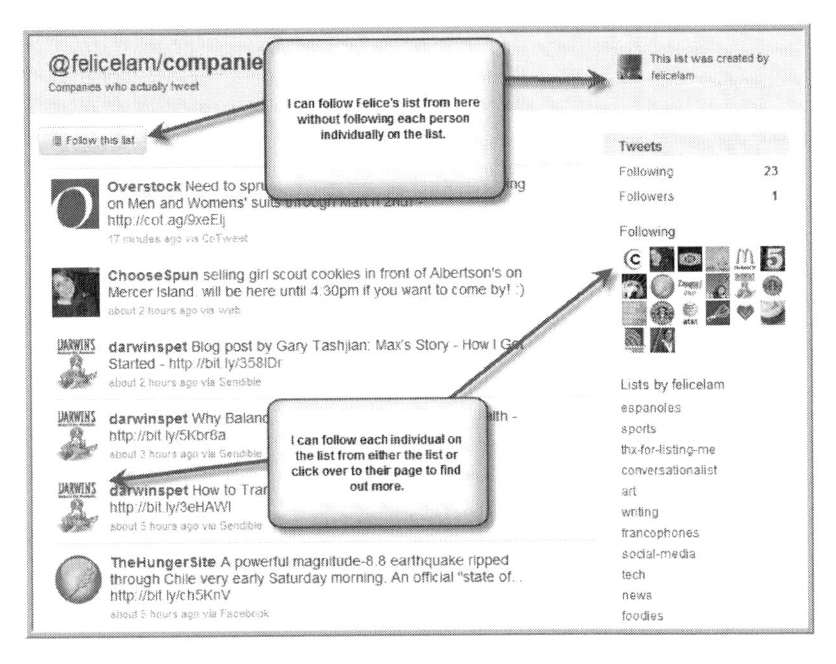

ONE OF @FELICELAM'S INDIVIDUAL LIST PAGES

There is also a "View Lists" link that takes you to the page of actual links on the page. It is at the bottom of all the lists in a person's profile. This takes you to a page that shows the lists that follow www.Twitter.com/felicelam and those that she follows.

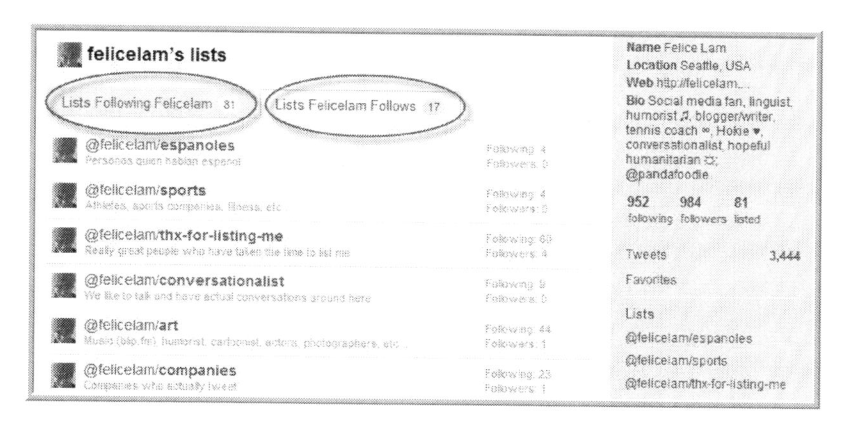

TWO LIST TABS – LISTS @FELICELAM FOLLOW AND THE LISTS FOLLOWING HER

Private lists will have a locked icon, but will be clearly evident on your page.

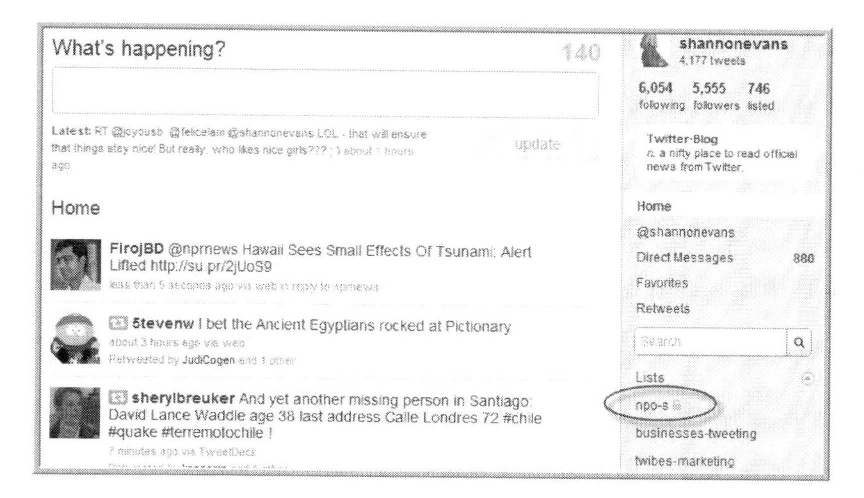

PRIVATE LIST WITH ALOCK SYMBOL

Have some care in naming your lists, so you do not alienate potential followers. You can edit the list, but if you change the list from Public to Private you will lose the followers. Changing from private to public makes the list open for anyone to follow.

EDIT/DELETE OPTIONS FOUND ON INDIVIDUAL LIST'S PAGE

To remove Twitter accounts from a list or to change the list they appear on, go to the list page where they appear and click on their profile icon.

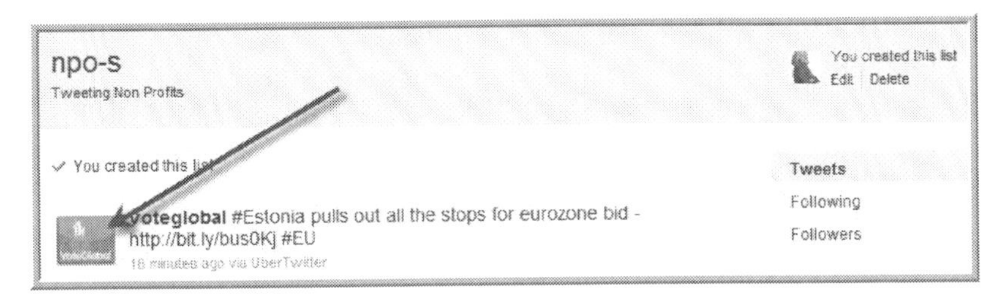

CLICK ON AVATAR

You will then be taken to their profile page and the list icon is on the right side of the page, just above their latest tweets. You can either follow/unfollow on the left or edit the lists the profiled user appears on.

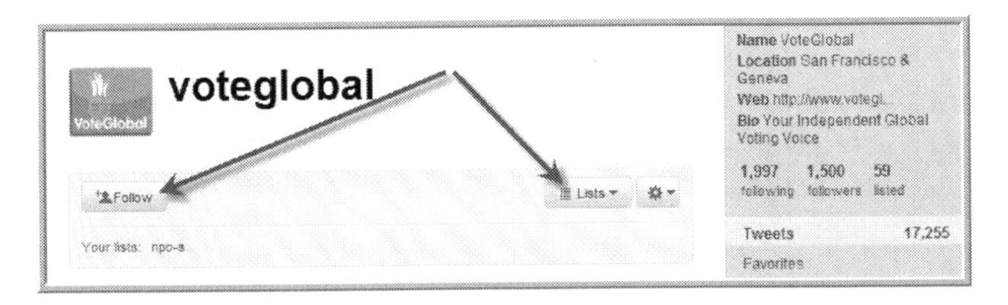

EDIT FROM THEIR PAGE

Click on the "Lists" button and simply uncheck the box next to the list name where you wish to remove them. You can also click additional boxes where you want to add them.

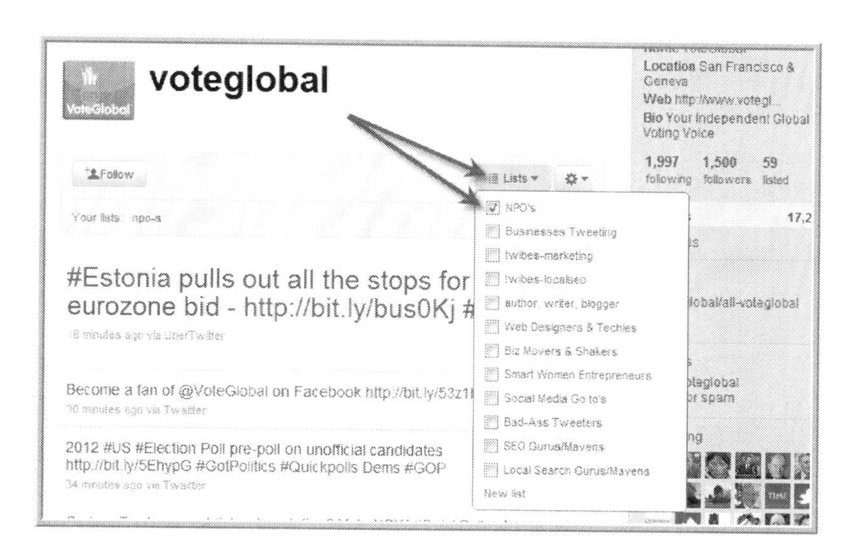

SELECT "LISTS" AND ADD OR EDIT THEIR INCLUSION ON YOUR LISTS

As you encounter new people to follow on Twitter, or perhaps you wish to observe others before you formally follow them, you can quickly and easily categorize them by adding each to a list. You can also find the lists they already appear on and scour them for leads for new people to consider observing, following and developing into valued members of your community.

Case Example: *Sandy Basker, Marketing Director of Nate Stories (therapeutic audio suggestion stories that empower children and parents to control behaviors like thumb sucking, bed wetting, etc), has found Twitter to be an invaluable prelaunch site for building momentum for her new product line. She (www.Twitter.com/natestories) began searching for people she wanted to follow and began with using keyword searches related to 'parenting'. Sandy quickly discovered the powerful world of mom bloggers. Sandy began to follow their follower/following as they were people most probably interested in parenting issues and topics. At about 600 follows, people started to find her. "It was at that point my follower list started to grow even when I didn't do anything on Twitter for a day or two." It was her 'critical mass' of sorts.*

@NATESTORIES TWITTER PAGE

Sandy began to develop lists of people she wanted to cultivate a relationship with, those she wanted to court to follow her back, and those she wanted to take a "wait and see" approach to following. She began to analyze those she followed to see who did not follow her back. If they had useful things to say and added value to her feed, she kept them on her list to monitor, though not to necessarily follow at this time. If she really wanted someone she followed to follow her back, she would find things they tweeted and retweet some of their useful material that usually motivates a follow back. She has also found that people often follow her because she appears on someone else's list.

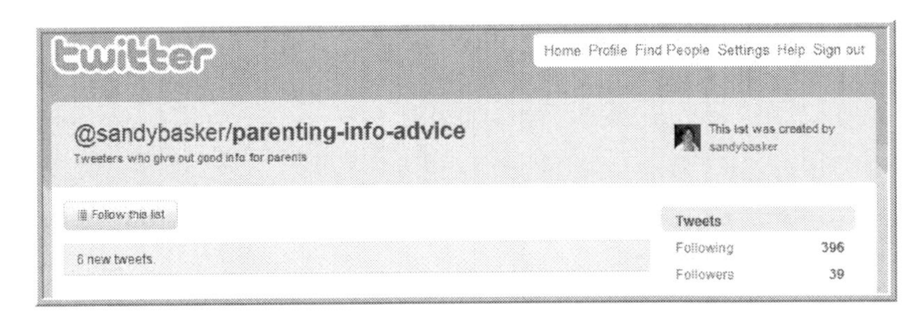

@SANDYBASKER LIST OF PARENT INFO ADVICE TWITTER ACCOUNTS

Sandy is also a huge advocate of tools like Tweepi to help her manage her follows. She looks for people with a high reach of influence and similar interests to explore who they follow and who follows them. She also uses it to flush inactive Twitter accounts, so she can free up space to add more people to her own follow list. "Overall," says Sandy, "Twitter and my lists are a great way to potentially take a message or a product viral. It is also a great way to find and group people with common interests. "

Lists are useful to create groupings of tweet feeds based on location, areas of interests, etc. It is a good way to recommend other Tweeps by promoting the list name in a tweet. Lists are a great way to take a quick peek at what those on the list are saying or doing without having to sort through the chaff of unrelated tweets.

If you want to follow lists others have created on which you are not included, you can still add them to the lists you follow. If you were from Seattle and you wanted to find others who were concerned about local news and events, you could follow lists that might include www.Twitter.com/news4seattle by first going to News4Seattle home page:

LINK TO @NEWS4SEATTLE LISTS WHERE THEY APPEAR

Click on the blue "listed" button on the right side of the page. This will take you to a page that shows lists following @news4seattle and those lists that News4Seattle follows.

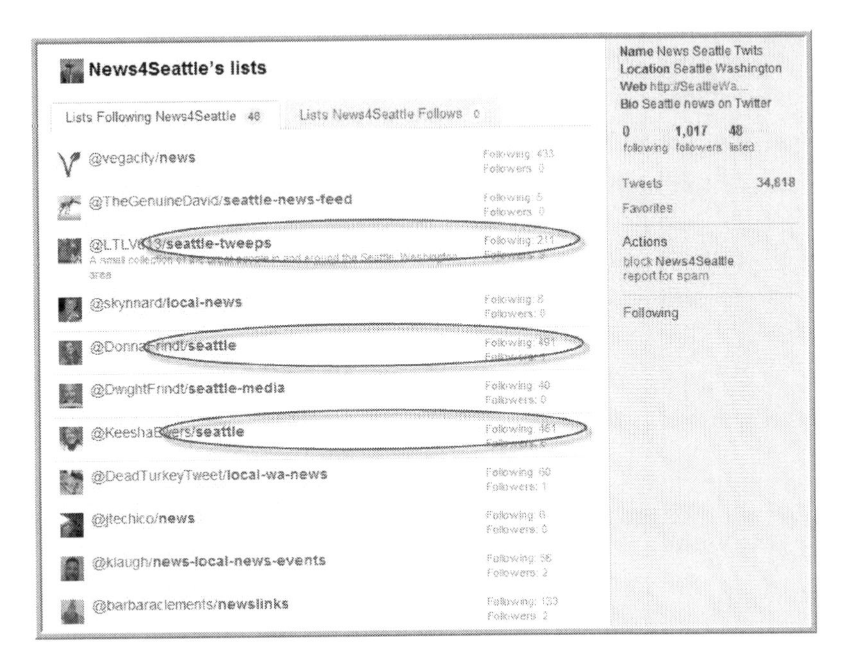

LISTS @NEWS4SEATTLE FOLLOWS

Notice how some of the lists are based on location Tweeters (www.Twitter.com/News4Seattle/seattle-tweeps, etc). If you were trying to build a local following, then these would be great lists to explore for new local followers, especially if you are trying to cultivate visits to a "brick and mortar" business.

Looking at the lists where News4Seattle appears there is one with a large number of Twitter accounts on the list titled 'donnafrindt/seattle'. Clicking over to her list reveals that there are almost 500 Twitter accounts included on her Seattle list.

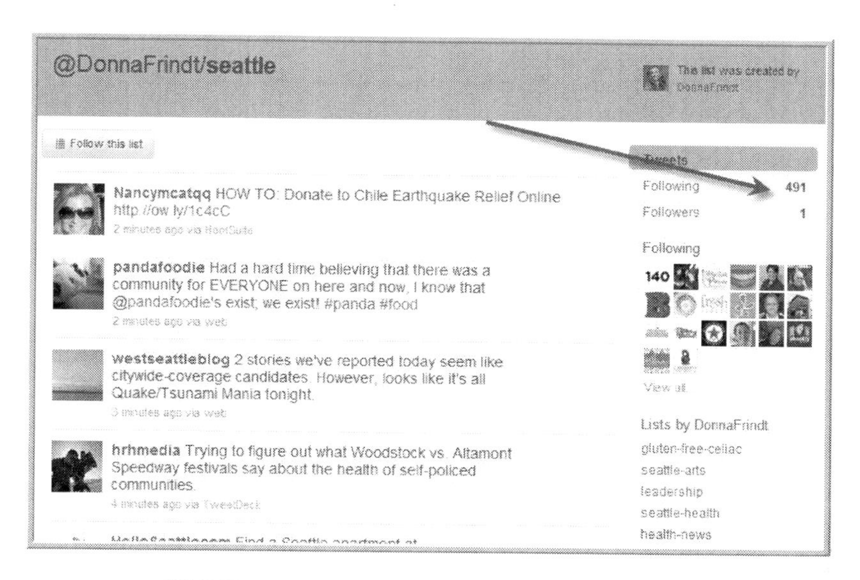

NUMBER OF FOLLOWERS OF @DONNAFRINDT'S SEATTLE LIST

At this point, you can choose to follow this list or select specific individuals to follow from the list.

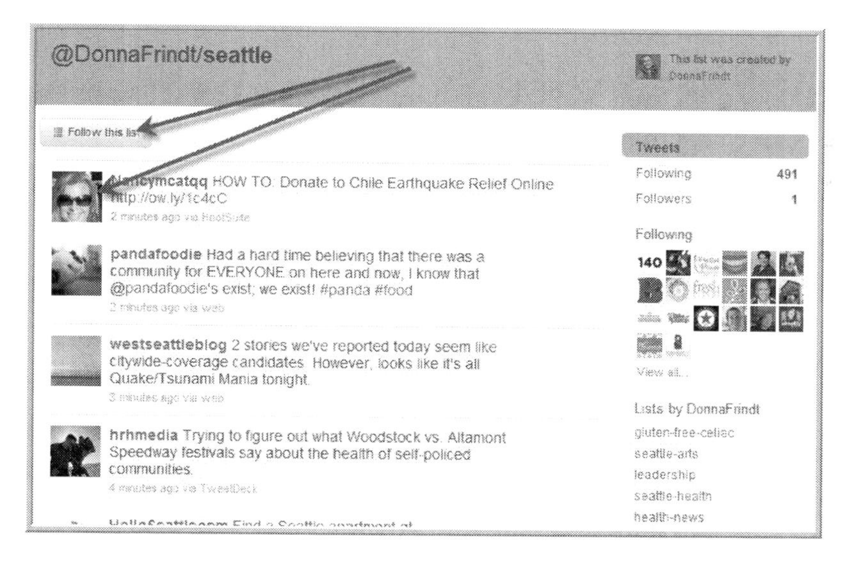

FOLLOW THE LIST OR SPECIFIC INDIVIDUALS ON THE LIST

Now let's assume that someone has placed you on a list you don't want to appear on ("rude-tweeters", "Bad-service", etc), you can remove your account from that list simply by blocking the owner of the list. This not only removes your account from the list, it prevents that person from following or DM'ing you as well.

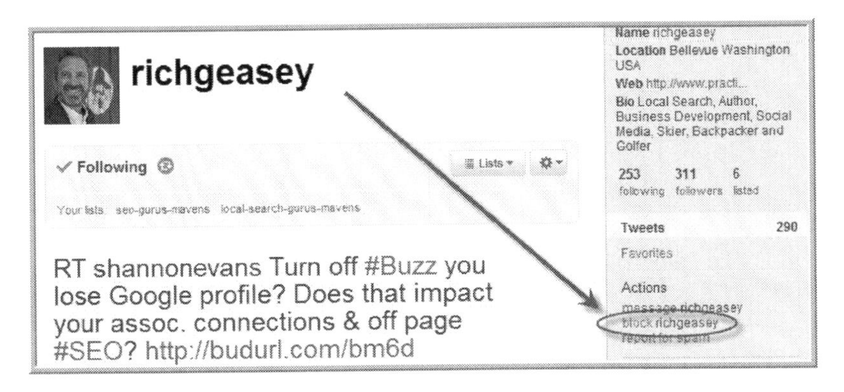

BLOCK AN ACCOUNT FROM THEIR PROFILE PAGE

You can also block and then unblock the person if you just want off the troublesome list!

Creating effective lists for marketing requires thinking tactically as well as strategically. Who is the target audience for this list? What do they look like? What are their needs? Is this a unique subset of your niche? What are their goals/objectives that I can help them meet with my tweets and through a cultivated online relationship? Does this niche 'hang out' on Twitter? What type of information do they share on Twitter and what do they seem to value? Thinking critically will help you create the lists that target each customer segment of your target audience.

For the sake of example, pretend that you are a dentist in New York City and you specialize in pediatric dentistry. Kids are not hanging out on Twitter…but the parents who ultimately chose the dentist often do! Your target audience might be the influential mommy bloggers who talk about children's health issues. What are the objectives of these moms who are the audience segment you want to target?

- Good health – of their family but more specifically their young children.
- Information about unique dental issues of young children
- Information on how to select between a general dentistry family oriented practice and a pediatric dentist
- Information about the unique skill sets of a pediatric dentist, their approach to dentistry, etc.
- Information on how to locate and validate a pediatric dentist nationally and locally.
- Information on what to expect on a first visit with a pediatric dentist, costs, insurance coverage, etc.

Find the mom bloggers and children's health Twitter accounts using Twitter's search function. Look for people tweeting your keywords (pediatric dentist, children's dentist, etc) and consider adding them to a list you create titled "NYC-Healthy-Kid-Teeth" or something keyword rich and catchy. Make your list a solution site for others who have similar interests and needs, watch your Twitter following and your business grow.

Case Example: *Affiliate marketers have found Twitter a useful place to track their customers and brand by topic. Twitter is a great pull marketing tool that is permission based. According to Jan Carroza (www.Twitter.com/social_dynamics) of Social Media Dynamics, (http://SocialMediadynamics.com) affiliate marketers now have the capability to build a list of all their affiliates in one place and to post a general notice to their entire list about a* *campaign's status. It is a rapid broadcast delivery system to announce changes, upgrades, or new competitions.*

JAN'S PROFESSIONAL TWITTER ACCOUNT

According to Jan, "Twitter offers a free haven for affiliates and managers to follow each other away from the filters that kept their legitimate email announcements from being delivered and an environment to share the latest news. They search the term "affiliate" to get more news and follow community leaders like Shawn Collins, publisher of the industry trade magazine, Feedfront." Twitter has become a powerful platform for affiliate marketers to congregate and learn from each other, and to also grow their businesses.

Once you have created your lists, don't forget to promote them off, as well as on, Twitter. Include links to your lists on your blog and in comments you leave on other blogs using: http://Twitter.com/your_name/yourlist_name. Promote your lists on Facebook, Hubpages, Squidoo Pages, and even in your company newsletters. Get out there and share this valuable resource with your customers and contacts.

There are currently three third-party sites that have their own directory of Twitter lists. It is a good idea to follow and even join:

Listorious: www.listorious.com has categorized lists of people on Twitter based on everything from location to humor and celebrity status.

Tweetmeme: www.tweetmeme.com has the most tweeted Twitter Lists featured on their site.

Twibes: www.twibes.com created by Adam Loving of Seattle,

Twibes is a way to create or follow groups or lists of people who have similar interests based on keyword tabs. Twibes vision is to help aggregate your Tweeps (followers) and manage a continuous discussion, create interactive pages, search by hashtags, and provide a view of comments on Twitter. It offers more than tools like WeFollow as Twibes lets you conduct a direct person search. The secondary benefit of Twibes is that it provides you with place holders for following specific tweets, a feed of tweets for relevant content, and a RSS feed source for information.

Choose the lists you want to create within Twitter carefully, as at this time you are limited to 20 lists per account. You can continually edit and delete them as your needs grow and change. Hopefully, as Twitter grows and changes to meet the needs of its users, it will allow you to create a default list to add all the unclassified people you want to observe or follow.

Tip: Use lists to:

- Monitor competitors and ‘experts’ in your industry.
- Create customer lists.
- Identify a niche.
- Make a directory.
- Categorize location-based Twitter accounts.
- Promote event attendees or vendors.
- Expose worthwhile groups, content, accounts, etc to your followers.
- Monitor new followers/followees you don’t want to immediately “lose” in the mix.

Chapter 9: How Do You Know If Your Twitter Efforts Are Working?

How do you monitor and measure the effectiveness of your Twittering? In traditional Internet marketing, companies count website click-thru actions and page views as a measure of effectiveness. Some companies even track the number of comments on a blog post as a metric. But that does not measure the depth or emotional charge of each individual comment. So how do you measure your marketing efforts and does social media even matter to marketing? Why bother monitoring social media?

Monitoring and participating in social media requires developing a tightly focused marketing strategy and then dedication to a long term marketing commitment. Participate in order to build brand reputation, learn who is talking about your brand or your niche, and then add to the conversation. Sounds simple! How do you know who's talking about you and who to follow on Twitter without making this into a full time job?

Twitter is a great way to get instant targeted feedback on specific sales and marketing campaigns. It is a cheap and effective way to get unsolicited opinions, and to identify and repair problems as they happen.

Use Twitter's search feature to see what people are saying and who is talking about you or your brand. Set up Google Alerts to have an automated feed of the latest discussions and articles about topics you are interested in, sent to your email daily.

How to Create Google Alerts

Go to http//:www.google.com/alerts. You will be directed to a page that has a form field on the right hand side for entering information to monitor.

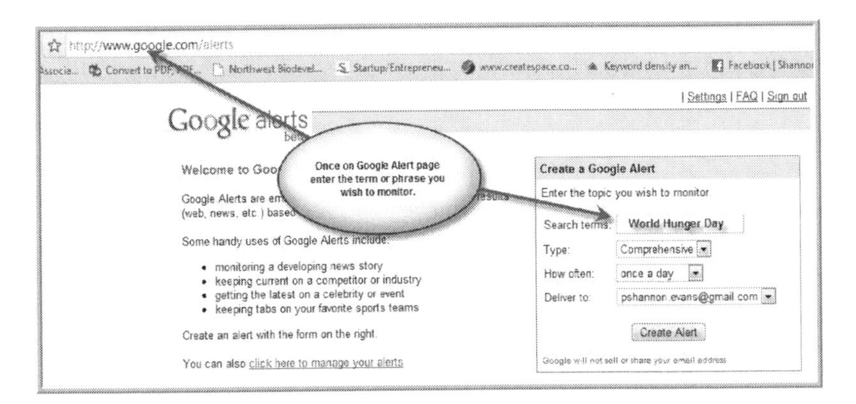

WWW.GOOGLE.COM/ALERTS HOME PAGE

Suppose the term "World Hunger Day" is the search term to be monitored. Google will return anything with "World" "Hunger" or "Day" in an article or news item indexed by the Google search engine. To make the information more focused, quotations can be used around the entire phrase to receive only information that has those three words presented in that exact phrase, somewhere in an article or news item.

You can determine the type of article or news item you would like to receive as well: news, blogs, Internet, video, or comprehensive. You can also determine the frequency with which you receive updates. The choices range from once a week to once a day.

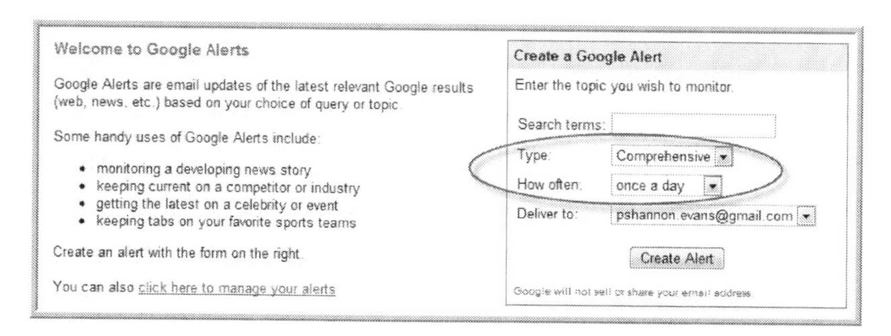

SELECT TYPE AND FREQUENCY OF ALERT TO BE DELIVERED

There is also a place to indicate which email address the alerts will be delivered to or you can direct the results to your Google Feed. The final step is to select "Create Alert" to launch your alert request.

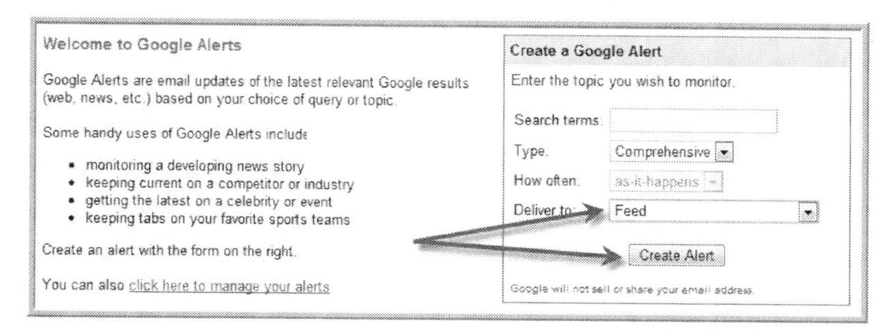

CREATE ALERT

You will then be taken to a message screen, indicating that your Google Alert has been created. You will receive a confirmation email asking you to verify the request for Google Alerts. Once verified, you will begin to receive an email digest of articles related to your alert request.

For the alert created for 'feed the hungry', the email digest delivered to your email will look like this:

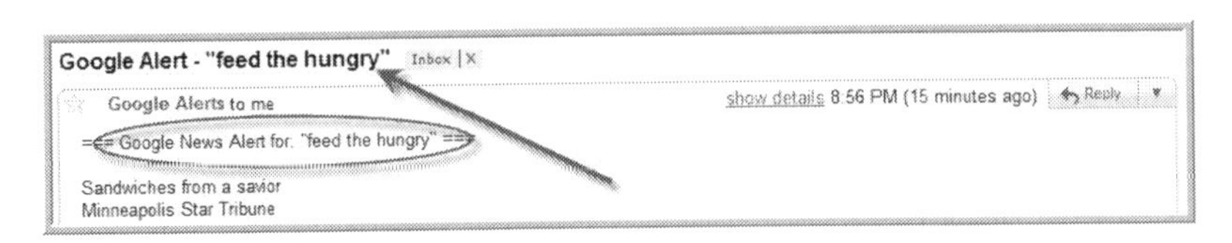

DELIVERY OF EMAIL DIGEST OF ALERT FOR "FEED THE HUNGRY"

To edit your Google Alerts, return to www.google.com/alerts and at the bottom of the welcome screen is the hyperlink titled "click here to manage alerts."

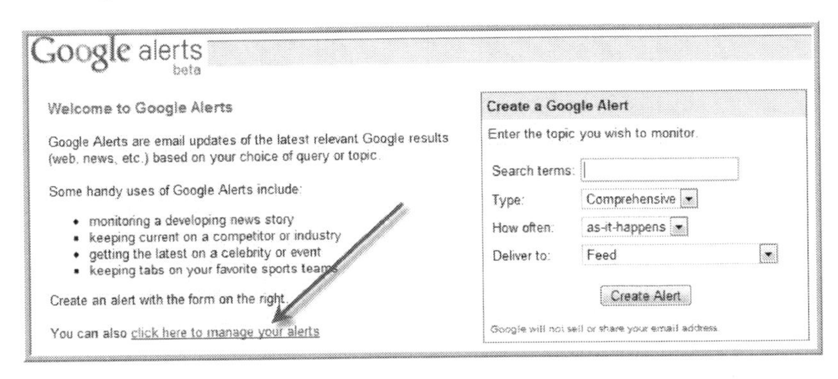

CLICK TO EDIT CURRENT GOOGLE ALERTS

This link will take you to a list of all your Google Alert accounts. Here you can edit your request or delete them entirely.

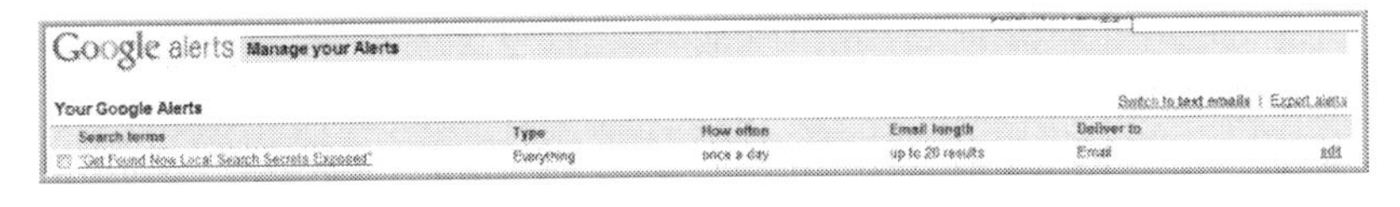

LIST OF ESTABLISHED GOOGLE ALERTS

What to Monitor with Google Alerts?

What do you actually monitor? What do you do with the information you get from Google Alerts? How the heck do you filter and make meaning of the different articles, tweets, and comments without experiencing information overload? Blog posts are often one of the most frequent sources of product or service feedback. Find what is said and decide if it warrants a company response or just watchful waiting. Product reviews are critical sources of information regarding public perception, viability, and customer endorsement of specific products.

USE TWITTER TO MONITOR BRAND MENTIONS

Twitter is another great place to track mentions of your brand, updates and trends in your industry, and to monitor your product or service for reviews.

Highly Targeted Twitter Accounts to Follow

Using Google Alert, you can research and pinpoint the specific Twitter accounts you want to reach out to; and perhaps engage in real conversations to foster as leads for business purposes. If you set up the right search query in your alerts, you will be able to grow your list rapidly and effectively.

So assume that you represent a software company that has a cool accounting tool with a new cell phone application and you want to find all the accountants on Twitter to cultivate as followers. You can create a Google Alert search string that is a bit more complicated, but easy to plug in:

> *intitle:"accountant * on Twitter" OR intitle:"accounting * on Twitter" OR intext:"bio accountant" OR intext:"bio accounting" OR intext:"bio * accountant" OR intext:"bio * accounting site: Twitter.com*

If you wanted to target tax accountants and CPA's, you could put in a more specific search string in your Google Alerts:

> *intitle:"tax accountant * on Twitter" OR intitle:"CPA * on Twitter" OR intext:"bio tax accountant" OR intext:"bio CPA" OR intext:"bio * tax accountant" OR intext:"bio * CPA site: Twitter.com*

If you are a local produce company who supplies restaurants and cafes locally, then a search on Twitter would take a more location specific approach:

> *intitle:"restaurant * on Twitter" OR intitle:"Cafe * on Twitter" OR intext:"bio restaurant" intext:"location Seattle" OR intext:"bio Cafe" intext:"location * Seattle" OR intext:"bio * restaurant" OR intext:"bio * Cafe site: Twitter.com*

If you construct detailed enough Google Alerts that match the pattern of Twitter page setups, you will know whenever a new Twitter account is created that matches your keywords and avoid getting unnecessary discussions that merely *contain* the keywords chosen. Finding highly targeted followers for your niche is far better than massively following random accounts that will never click over to your website or walk in your store.

Case Example: *Dee Gardner of DMG South (www.Twitter.com/DMGSouth) got involved with using Twitter when he had a customer who wanted to consider using Twitter. Dee found he was way behind the power curve on Twitter as a business and marketing tool, so he felt that in order to advise his customers, he better first become a user of the tool. He was amazed at some of the byproducts of opening a Twitter account, especially the significant increase in traffic to his company website www.dmgsouth.com.*

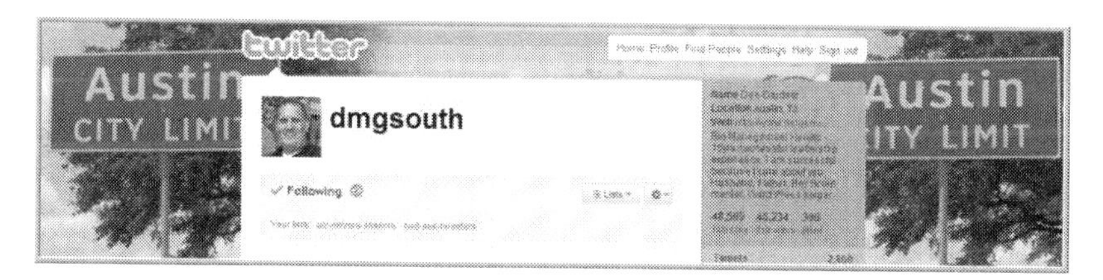

DMGSOUTH'S TWITTER ACCOUNT

In his local community, Austin, TX, his Twitter account has set him apart from others at networking events. People in the room, who follow him on Twitter, recognize his face before they ever meet him. They notice him both from his avatar (photo), and by his expertise that he shares through his Tweets. Dee has come to the conclusion that he cannot afford to stop Tweeting; he has become known locally as well as nationally, as an expert in his field. He also has found Twitter to be a huge library of information when he needs a resource. Dee finds Twitter so useful that he now actively tracks and monitors how it impacts his own business as well as that of his clients.

What to Measure

There are those who say that social media has no real measurable outcomes associated with it and therefore, worthless to the serious marketer. There are some specifically measurable elements and some terrific web tools to measure specific objectives. Some are free and some can be really pricey! But what do these tools actually track and measure? Here are a few:

- Number of blog visitors.
- Number of friends/connections on Facebook or LinkedIn.
- Number of followers on Twitter.
- Number of times your website has been clicked over to from your social media landing page.
- Number of visitors who download your articles, photos, links, etc.
- Number of mentions you get in a Tweet.
- Number of times other bloggers mention you or your product/goods/service.
- Keywords used to find you.
- Frequency or trending of specific keywords or phrases.

By understanding how to measure and what to measure for your brand, you can begin to follow your success easily and quickly on each social platform. This isn't rocket science; my teenager figured out social media faster than he did his new game controllers!

Large corporations have already figured out that they need to monitor social media for people talking about them, the industry, personal experiences with their products, etc. Where many of these companies fail is that they forget that social media is about conversation and not a one-way dialogue. When a company begins to think contextually about the conversations already occurring on Twitter, they begin to see the potential for lead generation, customer service outreach, future customers, and the list goes on.

Case Example: *David Schaefer is the Director of Public Relations at the Woodland Park Zoo in Seattle, WA. He deals with community and public relations on a daily basis. Woodland Park has had on and off again relations with the neighbors surrounding the zoo, due to parking and traffic woes. David and his staff work continually to foster good relations with the community. The zoo grounds and buildings are owned by the city of Seattle while the Woodland Park Zoo Foundation owns the animals. For the zoo to stay open, they need funding from King County Parks Commission which requires city council funding.*

The zoo houses an elephant exhibit which resulted in the highly touted public birth of baby Hamsa. The elephant exhibit has continually been under pressure from elephant rights activists, who absolutely hate any elephant living in a zoo and some of the techniques various animal handlers use with elephants. In some facilities with elephants, bull hooks are used to manage the large animals. At Woodland Park, they are not used nor are the keepers allowed in with the elephants. They prefer to respect that elephants are wild animals and should not be turned into pets trained to do 'tricks'. Then their much touted, much loved Hamsa, the baby elephant died. It was a crushing blow to the Zoo and to the local community.

This caused an outcry from activists around the world and created a PR nightmare for the zoo. As a non-profit, they had a huge problem to address and discovered that they had to really concentrate their resources on addressing concerns over the Internet. It completely changed their marketing and communication approach.

As an organization, the Woodland Park Zoo has created a company social media policy for specific topics like funding and the elephants. As a result of changes in communication styles in Seattle and the growing world of social media, zoo community outreach has evolved. They are proud to be the first zoo known to have their own iPhone app! The zoo has hired a social media outreach person, who was comfortable with technology, has a BS in Biology, and a background in working with non-profit organizations.

Members of the zoo can respond independently on Twitter, but if the subject is a current 'hot' topic or is potentially controversial, they have to run blog posts past either the Director of Public Affairs or Animal Experts on staff. They have a really active Twitter account as well:

WOODLAND PARK ZOO TWITTER PAGE

Recently, the zoo announced the closing of the Nocturnal House exhibit. There was no press release about the closing, as it was in the zoo's annual plan. Scott Gifford, a local attorney posted on Facebook that this closure was a terrible thing to happen to the zoo. He formed a fan page to try and save the exhibit.

A WOODLAND PARK ZOO NOCTURNAL HOUSE FAN PAGE CREATED BY A LOCAL CITIZEN

Unfortunately, the exhibit had to close due to internal issues related to worker injury complaints. There are issues that can only be resolved with a complete rebuild of the structure that houses the exhibit. Undeterred, the Facebook fans raised $5000 in a week. Fortunately, the zoo and the fans have joined forces and are working together to use the funds to move most of the animals to another exhibit hall. The zoo was quick to recognize the strength of social media to inform and to form public opinion.

Twitter has become a favorite tool of public affairs at the zoo. They used Twitter and many other information methods to inform the public that a monkey had escaped. Dave found out that the monkey had escaped first because he saw a Tweet that said people should go into buildings at the zoo. Then he heard news helicopters overhead. David was amazed by the power of social media and the antics of a single monkey.

"As Twitter has grown in popularity it is interesting to see what have been the most popular topics at the zoo: Which animal is having sex and who's pooping where. Perhaps the funniest long term discussions on Twitter related to the zoo has been about a pair of ostriches that were brought to the zoo as a mating pair. Unfortunately, they were both females! Apparently, according to veterinarians, determining the sex of these large birds is not so easy,

'Ostriches don't really like you checking them out for gender!' Who knew?"

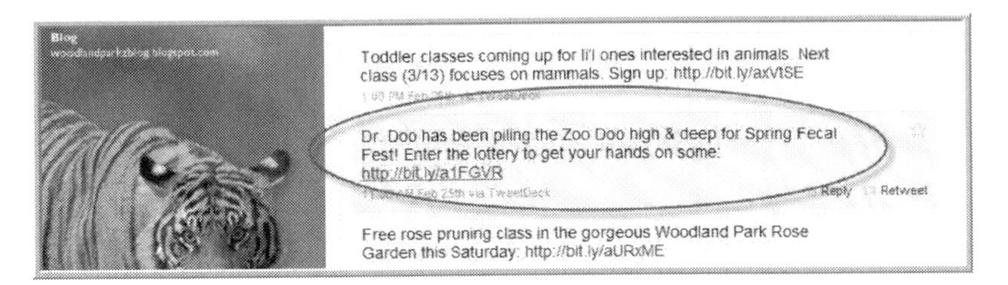

WOODLAND PARK ZOO'S TWITTER PAGE

Woodland Park Zoo is a great example of an organization trying to create a more personalized relationship for their audience. They found that it was important for them to identify their audience and figure out where they "hang out", so they could reach out to them and connect with them. While the zoo is not a traditional small business, they use the same PR techniques that small businesses use on a daily basis. According to David, they are keenly aware that they need a social presence and not just a website in today's market.

Small businesses can now be on the leading edge of their industry using tools like Twitter to reach out to their existing and potential clients/customers.. Social media has made it possible to put a face on a brand. No one wants to talk to a faceless entity. They want to talk to a real person and Twitter fortunately lets you put a name and a 'voice' to you and your brand.

Start by measuring three to four touch points that tie to your goals and objectives. In many cases, the number of followers you have is irrelevant. What is in fact the measure of your success is connected to your Voice and the Sentiment surrounding your brand. Once you build your Twitter community, how many actually read your blog and comment? Can you test responses to your tweet? How do your followers feel about your competition? Are you just responding to crisis contacts? Are you creating 'stories' that resonate with your audience? Monitor what is important to your business' growth and track it over the long term.

Search Engine Optimization and Twitter

Optimizing content on the web is essentially the same for blogs, video, images, and Twitter. While the platforms for delivery may vary, the need for highly targeted keyword use is critical to Search Engine Optimization (SEO) success.

Social media sites are highly trusted sites that search engines tend to rank highly. Highly optimized business profiles on sites like Twitter, Facebook, and LinkedIn that are frequently updated with fresh material will attract search engines often. To get the most out of social media means you must start out with an effective profile that uses the right keywords for search engines to find you.

When the right keywords are used in title tags, meta tags and content, the results are phenomenal. Inbound links and cross links occur. Search based traffic explodes, and brand visibility grows. Leveraging keywords in social media to your brand's benefit is just as important and actually quite easy.

For SEO purposes, if you want to rank for your business name you want to use the correct anchor text. CluePad is a company name, not Clue_Pad or Clue-Pad, etc. Your title tag if done correctly will show up in search and will look like this for your Twitter account:

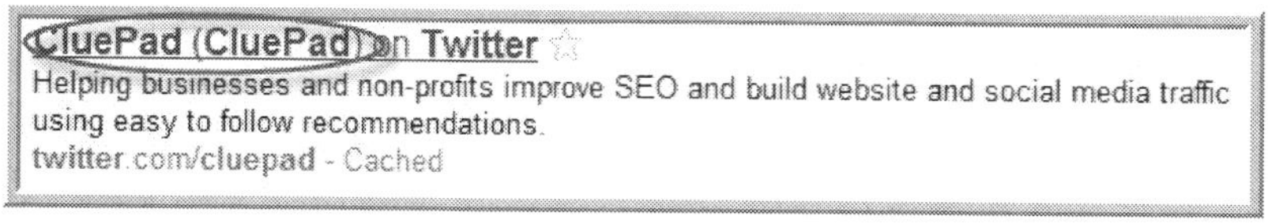

CluePad (CluePad) on Twitter
Helping businesses and non-profits improve SEO and build website and social media traffic using easy to follow recommendations.
twitter.com/cluepad - Cached

GOOGLE SEARCH RESULTS

To adjust how your Twitter title tag shows up in search go to your Twitter profile page and select "Settings" and change your "Name" (but not your "Username").

The information under your Twitter title tag is taken directly from your Twitter bio. It is the meta description that search engines and Twitter directories provide for readers to figure out what the listed site is all about…so make them count! It is interesting to note how many Twitter business profiles either ignore the bio box as a great place to leave a keyword rich description of their goods and services or pack it with unrelated information. To edit your Twitter bio, select "Settings" and change your bio.

Profile: Use niche specific keywords and localized keywords where appropriate.

In Profile:

KEYWORDS IN BIO

In posts:

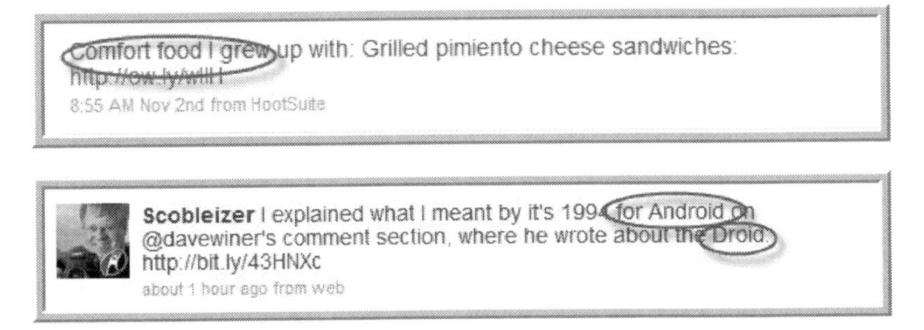

KEYWORDS IN POSTS

There is a direct correlation between the popularity of keywords, good content, and the increase in relevant inbound links to your site. Use the right keywords for your audience, provide content that encourages sharing and linking, and you will begin to see positive results rapidly. SEO and Social Media Marketing attract links that directly improve your visibility.

Converting the Information into Something Useful

Understanding who is visiting your website, how they got there, and the keywords they used to find you is critical to successful marketing in social media. Perhaps the most important metric of all is how you were found. Was it through specific keywords related to your brand? Was it your actual brand name? Knowing how you were found and followed or "friended" is invaluable data. If you know the keywords people used to find your profile or website, you can then figure out how to leverage those keywords in your brand's social media profile, your posts, and even in the images you post on video/imaging sharing sites.

Case Example: *Book Pal Bulk Books President, Tony Dicostanzo uses Twitter for SEO as a means to propel further growth and broaden the scope of their business base. Twitter is a great tool for them to garner useful back links for their site* http://www.book-pal.com/ *and to lead readers to their* http://bookpalblog.com/ *site as well.*

@BOOKPAL_US OFFICIAL TWITTER PAGE

They have used a combination of efforts on their website, blog, and Twitter to rank on the first page of Google search results for several of their keywords. This interweaving of their efforts across their various Internet platforms has helped them grow their following. They have made publishers, authors, and other publishing industry related professionals aware of Book Pal Bulk Books (www.Twitter.com/bookpal_us).

If you master the keyword search game, you have the potential to populate the entire first page of search results for those terms on Search Engines with your website, your Tweets, your blog entries, and your images/videos.

Time Warp of Social Media

Managing your time and your "friends" on social media can be overwhelming and consume a lot of time if you do not have goals and strategies to reach your target audience. Setting specific measurable goals and objectives help; but you first have to know your target audience:

- What are their social networking behaviors?
- What type of content do they like?
- How do they like to be presented with information?
- Where do they spend their time online?

Once you decide who and where your audience is, you have to select who you want to follow and interact with and then manage those relationships. How do you decide who to follow and who to not follow? Making friends is no different online then it is in person. You don't go to a convention or trade show, collect 100 business cards and then count all those people as your friends. The same is true in social networking.

Do NOT follow 100 random strangers at a time. Do it carefully and judiciously. Stop, look and listen to what people are saying in your niche. Make sure the potential "follower" is actively participating on the site. Analyze their comments on Twitter for appropriateness. Do they have a fairly complete profile? Visit their website and learn a little about them and their business before following.

When it comes to receiving a "follow back" request caution is the word of the day as well! Check out their profile and learn about them first. Spammers are notorious for having little or no information about themselves and no avatar (photo). Use caution when accepting their "friendship". If they are someone you would not let your mom or sister talk to online, you probably should not either. Choose carefully. The person with the most friends does NOT win a prize.

"Everyone is a friend, until they prove otherwise."

Unknown

Chapter 10: Manage And Measure With Third Party Tools

There are various tools out there for managing your social media efforts with a sales or marketing team. Most users of Twitter want to track visitors, leads, referrals, and conversion to customer. But how do you do that and what tools do you use? How do you know how effective you are with your tweets?

What to Measure

So what are some of the things you want and need to measure to determine the effectiveness of your marketing efforts on Twitter? Some of what you will need to measure is in Twitter itself and some will be measured from your website. Some basic information is easiest to quantify no matter the social networking platform. Tracking visitors is easy to quantify:

Followers: Track how many unique new followers you have per day/per country/per tweet account.

Log-ins: Each individual follower's total number of log-ins, their most recent log-in, and time elapsed between log-ins.

Posts: Total number of posts, type of posts, post length, content, number of posts flagged for spam, and number of posts with commentary.

Visits: Unique visitors, amount of time they spend viewing your Tweets per visit, frequency and number of return visitors, depth of visit to your website or links from Twitter.

But how do you track leads? What type of information is indicative of lead potential? How does a business decide where to invest their time in Twitter and how do they determine what is working and what isn't? A clear business strategy is critical to any marketing efforts. Social media marketing is no different. You must have a unique selling position (USP), a clear set of goals and objectives for your marketing efforts, as well as definite milestones in place, regardless of your marketing forum. As Yogi Berra says, "If you don't know where you're going you will end up somewhere else!"

> ***Tip***: Add a Twitter "Follow Me" Badge to your Website.
>
> On Twitter at the bottom of your home page is a navigation bar with some useful tips, links, and tools. Click on the "Goodies" link and you will go to a page where you can get widgets and "follow me" buttons for your website.
>
> A widget is a piece of code that shows your Twitter feed directly on your website. The "follow me" button is a piece of code that allows visitors on your website to click from your website page over to your Twitter profile and follow you.
>
> This provides another way to encourage your customers to interact with you!

Tracking leads does you no good if you are not absolutely clear where you are trying to lead your followers. While Twitter participants don't like to be sold, they do like valuable information. When they do make that leap to click over to your site from the link in your Twitter profile, you must have not only the right landing page (target site where you are sending your followers) and content, but the tools in place to measure what happens once they get there.

Tools like Google Analytics (free) and Powershift from Radian6, Techrigy, Trackur, and BuzzMetrics from Nielsen help to measure everything from passive activity (like page views) to contributory activity like opting in for information, or membership and commenting on content on your website.

Some of the most useful information that you can track and measure is time. Track the time your visitors spend on your website, the total time per page, and the frequency of each individual's visit. The depth of visit on your site will help you determine what values to assign to each page and what content is most popular with your niche. This helps you to be more proactive in creating unique content and to moderate for comments, etc. When visitors to your site find good content that is stimulating, thought provoking, or uniquely fits their needs, they tend to react to it by reposting to their blog, website, or even posting a link to their own Twitter following. This creates recursive SEO power for you and your website. There is a direct correlation that can be made between good content and user engagement.

Gist: A Monitoring and Transmission Management Tool

One tool that is really great for managing all your social media contacts, email contacts and prospects in one place is Gist. Gist is a resource management tool that helps companies "accelerate their prospecting, create new PR opportunities, and engage their customers" all from one convenient dashboard interface program.

Gist is useful to those who manage more than one social media account by aggregating all the contact information and details in one central location; it shows you all the people you are connected with and how they interact with you. This frees you to spend less time looking for information on a prospect and lets you spend more time acting on a lead or engaging with the customer or prospect. You spend a lot less time sorting.

Gist allows you to filter Tweets from your most important customers. With Gist, you can share a Tweet via email to a highly targeted list across multiple platforms including, but not limited to

Facebook, LinkedIn, email, Google, and even Salesforce.com, so you can amplify messages. This is highly relevant for small business owners, since it not only creates a simplified cross platform management tool, but it also provides a means for tracking traffic efficiently. Gist lets you sort accounts by people, by company, and by industry, allowing multiple levels of tracking and monitoring. Gist lets you customize feeds for customer relevance, track your contacts' traffic, respond efficiently to your network, and give an increased ability to filter to acquire industry news.

Use the Gist dashboard to help identify potential leads, new customers, and to cultivate relationships that you start on Twitter. Customer relationships are built on a cumulative effect. Paying particular attention to conversations, expanding them through private messages and then with email, can have long lasting impact on your business.

Some Measurement Tools to Explore

One of the first things I tell existing users of Twitter to do is to first have a look at where they are and then determine where they want to end up. A good pre-test measure of your existing account can be done using the following tools:

http://twitalyzer.com

http://Twittergrader.com/

Twitalyzer is a free analytical tool that evaluates individual user's Twitter efforts. This great tool evaluates the users:

- 'Clout': likelihood of user name showing up in search.
- 'Generosity': frequency of retweeting others.
- 'Engagement': ratio of references, followers and following.
- Influence: likelihood of being retweeted.

- Impact: an amalgam of various indicators that include followers, retweets, frequency of posts, etc.

Twitalyzer is a useful tool for analyzing your impact on the world of Twitter. The results might surprise you! Based on Twitalyzer's algorithm tools, you can figure out how you compare with other Twitter users.

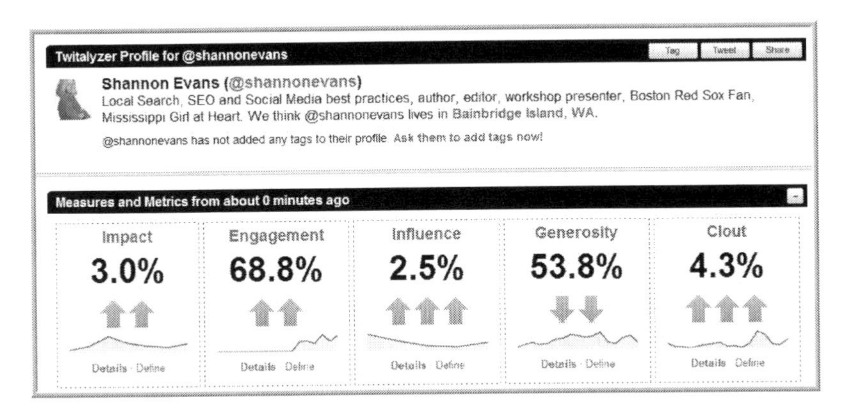

TWITALYZER EVALUATION

Twitalyzer can be used to help you measure your tendency to share good information rather than garbage. This is measured by the number of references you make to other people with the use of the "@" symbol, the links to URLs you share, as well as the hashtags and retweets of other tweeter's information.

Go to your Twitalyzer dashboard to see more specific details that give you a better understanding of how you are doing with your Twitter account.

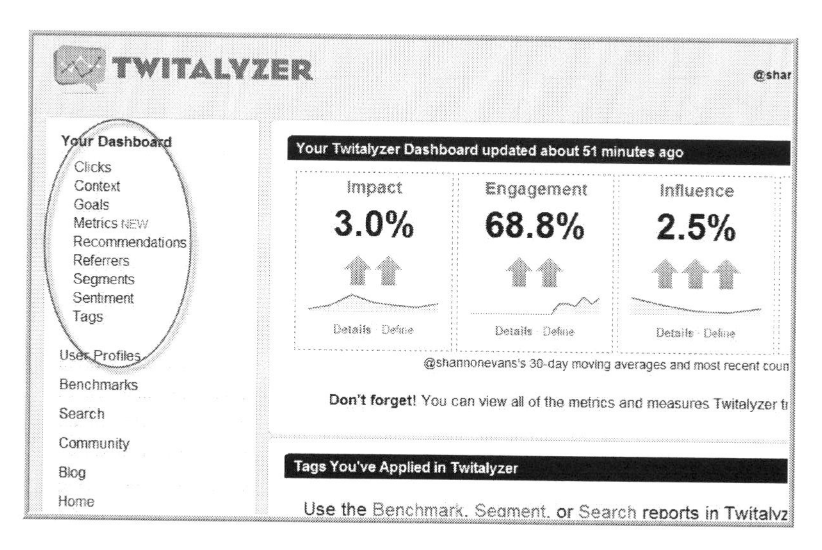

The *Clicks* report examines the shortened URLs (via Bit.ly or Budurl, etc) you share from your account and their associated individual click thru rate. *Context* is your impact on the Twitterverse compared to all other users. The *Goals* feature allows you to set your own performance targets. *Metrics* include anything you can possibly measure of merit on Twitter from 'impact' to 'hashtags' used. *Recommendations* provide a detailed list of actions you can take to improve your Tweeting and your results on Twitalyzer. *Segment* is similar to creating groups or lists. This allows you to follow tagged individuals en bloc either by topic or keyword. *Sentiment* is a report that analyzes the positive and negative language that appears in conversations. The filter is editable, so if the word "bad" is good in your circle of friends; you will want to make some customized changes to the filter.

Twitter Grader (www.twittergrader.com) is a free tool that analyzes how much influence you have on Twitter compared to all other users. Simply log on to their website and enter your user name (Twitter Handle) or anyone else's name you want to assess and then click "Grade":

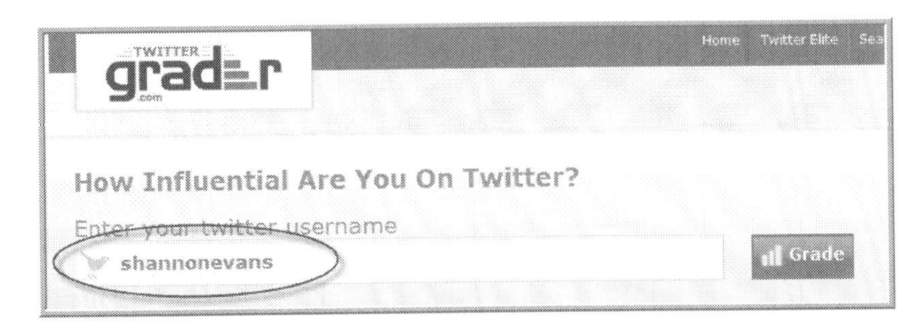

TWITTER GRADER

A results page will be returned that gives you a grade, just like in school, where a score under 70 is still less than passing! You can see the ranking of the profile analyzed compared to the other 6, 000,000 + analyzed by Twitter Grader.

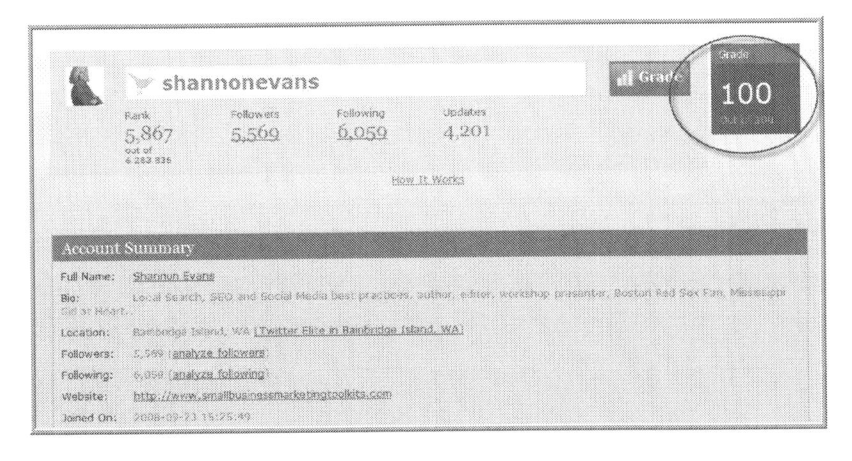

TWITTER GRADER RESULTS

These two simple tools provide an excellent analysis of where you stand and how you compare to others in your niche, locale, and in the "Twitterverse" at large.

How To Gather and Use Twitter Metrics

Metrics on Twitter are nothing more than numbers related to Twitter that help you to figure out exactly where you stand in the social media community of Twitter. They help you to evaluate a specific campaign or discussion on Twitter. So how do you do that? How do you measure your efforts on social media and Twitter more specifically? Let's look at it first from the big picture of your Twitter account and then dig down to the campaign level.

Follower Count Metrics: When you look at the more global metrics of Twitter, you want to first look at your follower count.

FOLLOWER/FOLLOWING COUNT

Look at your name on the top right of the Twitter screen. You will see your location, website, bio, etc followed by the number of people you are following and the number of people who follow you. As a company, it is ideal to have over 1000 followers. As your numbers increase, your consumer awareness factors increase as well. If there is a large difference between your followers and who you are following, some filters can block you as a potential "spammer". Keep the relationship between the two numbers relatively close so you attract savvy Tweeters.

If you follow quality people and engage them in conversation, you will open many more new opportunities for networking and brand building.

A useful site for analyzing your follower count is Twitterholic. Twitterholic shows your account over time in relationship to the number of new followers and followees you have. It also ranks you compared to a specific region or area. While not totally accurate in its number count, it is still a good gauge of you compared to your local (geographic) competition.

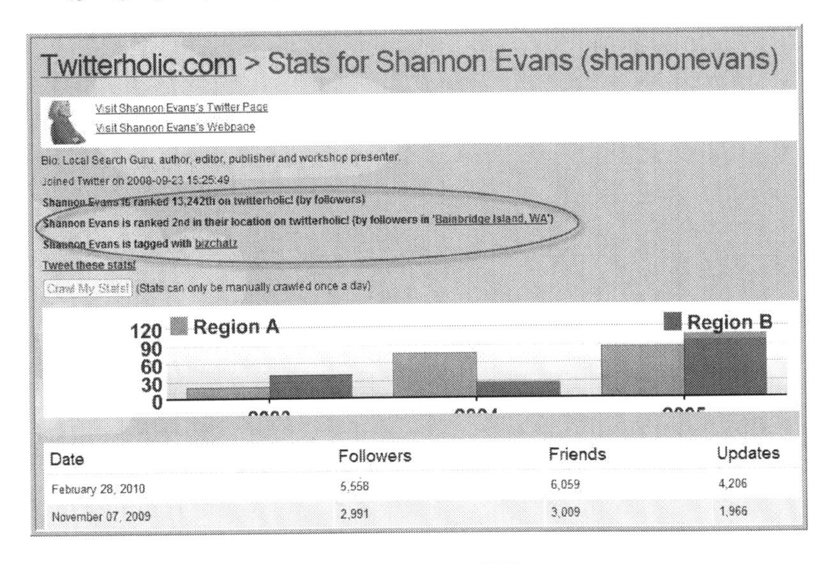

TWITTERHOLIC RESULTS

If you are truly a local brand and need to monitor a much tighter geographic Twitter following, you will want to check out Nearbytweets.com. This is a great geo-centric tool for building local customer relationships and monitoring brand mentions in real time. It allows businesses to monitor not only brand buzz, but to connect with customers, as well as to create Twitter-based promotional. It is also a useful tool for crisis management or customer service issues and for finding other locals on Twitter!

At the end of the day, there are three things you want to measure on social media whether it is for a local or a global campaign:

- Objectives
- Output
- Outcomes

Let's take a simple example of a social media campaign and flesh it out according to the above three criterion. For the sake of example, you are a small boutique that sells specialty high end women's custom fitted clothing in a major metropolitan community. Assume you already have a Twitter account, a website with a blog, and an existing client (e)mail list. Your objective is a new fall line of clothing that you really want to move this month. First, you write a brief article for your blog that talks NOT about the new fall line in particular, but about the colors that are "hot," or the new hemlines that are "in" or about a facet of the new line of clothing that will draw interest from your readers.

Pay particular attention to the use of specific keywords to use in the blog title and the blog content to make it search engine friendly. Then expand that blog post content into a press release to promote the new style and why it is newsworthy. Then post a full-fledged article that focuses on the same keywords and includes a link to your blog and your Twitter account to post in an ezine article repository. Now you have to sprinkle in the social media elements. In between your tidbits of industry news and retweets you post, share a link to your blog with a brief lead in that makes people WANT to click over. When the press release gets picked up and posted, share that link with your followers. Once your article goes live on the ezine site, share the link with your followers as well. If you do all of this repeatedly, over time you will begin to generate some real traffic.

When the traffic starts to come in from various sources, trace that output for effectiveness and efficacy. What type of traffic do you get to your website? How many new Twitter followers do you get who arrive from the article? By looking at the referring sites and how viewers arrive at your website -either from social media, the press release, or the article – you will be able to begin to measure the output of your campaign.

Case Example: *Chris Kelly, owner of Stellar Skin Salon and Hair Salon Spa and Beauty Biz Builder (www.Twitter.com/beautybizbuildr), observed that the most successful members of her mindset mastermind group was Twittering on a regular basis. Whether they were solo-entrepreneurs or big business executives, they were actively on Twitter creating relationships and making connections. They even let their followers see their 'real life' warts and all, not just the 'business as usual' side of their personalities. Chris loves Twitter because, "you can glance and move on! I started Tweeting and noticed an immediate measurable impact on my business."*

Chris has linked her blog to her Twitter account and has designed it so that her followers on her Facebook Fanpage know that she also has a Twitter page. She has implemented a few tools to automate some of her tasks as she is a successful business woman and mother of three busy children. She has her marketing, current promotions, and general information Tweets set up before the week begins. This leaves her free to answer questions, interact personally, and cultivate relationships on Twitter in her spare time on her iPhone. Chris adds, "It works for you while you are off making money or hitting a golf ball. And the best part is it is free! Twitter is a great way to start getting to know those you want to know. Twitter your business to success, I am!"

To measure the outcomes, you will want to ask every customer who comes in how they found you. Write it down! On your website watch for comments, check your emails and monitor your phone calls. How many of them were a direct result of the campaign? If you do not get the traffic you expected, perhaps you should revisit the keywords you used. They may have been good keywords, but not the ones your customer segment uses in search. With some basic research and investigation, you can tweak your campaign and re-measure in your next attempt. Don't be afraid to add your Twitter badge to your blog, website, Facebook fanpage, or your articles. You want to be found and followed!

The bottom line is that Twitter is a low cost effective marketing tool to have in your toolbox! Here are a few extra tips to help increase your conversion rates online:

Make your website's landing page trustworthy. Don't have a cheesy sales page full of ads and discounts on your homepage. Add testimonials, company achievements and awards. Make your business one they want to visit. Display your address and contact information, if appropriate.

Twin Cities Cheap (@twincitiescheap) posts their exclusive discounts on Twitter for local businesses. They advertise individual coupons that are on their website www.twincitiescheap.com with a direct link to each business' 'splash' page on the website.

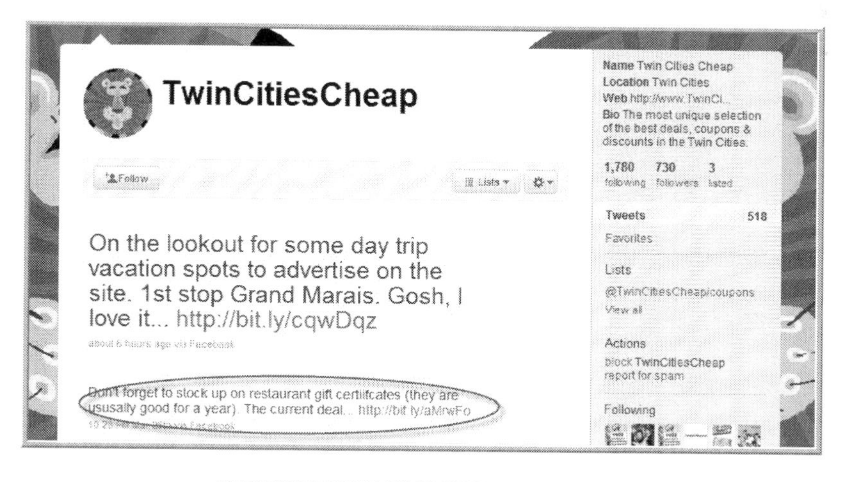

@TWINCITIESCHEAP'S PROMOTIONAL TWEETS

Offer products your customers are looking for and expect. Do not sell rakes and shovels if you are a shoe store! Highlight your discounted offerings on your website. Don't make your visitor hunt...or they will leave! Offer time limited sales discounts and promotions. Make sure you have a clearly visible and NON-pushy call to action on your website. If you sell goods/services online, make checkout as easy and painless as possible and sell from the appropriate pages of your website…not from your Twitter account!

If you have a blog, don't just pump out an automated RSS feed onto Twitter. Engage, converse, and share...and then have a convincing and trustworthy website that keeps them coming back again and again.

Case Example: *Kerianne Mellott (@Keri_Mellott), owner of MarketingMakesMeSmile.com, is a marketing coach from Los Angeles, CA who uses Twitter extensively as a tool for her business. Kerianne teaches business owners to create a marketing foundation for their business first in order to identify a targeted niche audience. Only then can you begin to shape your brand and your marketing message and measure its impact. Her emphasis in her own business is to be 100% authentic, but remain cautious about what is said so that nothing comes across "spammy" or "salesy". She employs the 80-20 rule: 80% personal updates to 20% promotional information.*

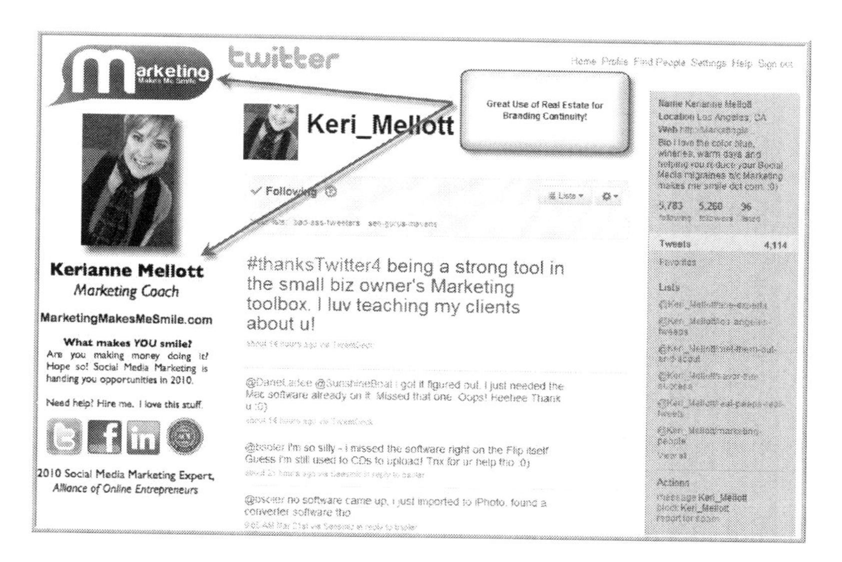

KERIANNE MELLOTT HIGHLY CUSTOMIZED TWITTER PROFILE

@Keri_Mellot's customized background makes good use of precious real estate; it helps people to find her as well as to promote brand continuity for MarketingMakesMeSmile.com. Twitter use has directly impacted her business by getting new clients and cultivating new business relationships. According to Kerianne, "I have grown my business more rapidly since using Twitter as a tool to find information more rapidly and then deliver it to my clients. It is amazing how quickly I can build relationships on Twitter compared to face to face meetings. I have used Twitter to discover new prospects, cultivate joint ventures, and to find related business websites I might never have landed on otherwise. I track all my contacts and am constantly amazed at the direct impact Twitter has on my business."

Business Metrics For Individual Twitter Followers

There are some basic metrics for social media that all businesses should monitor and perhaps even track for determining the impact they are having in a particular niche.

Case Example: *Awareness, Inc works with businesses that are trying to have continuous branding across all their social media platforms and to help them build real online communities (www.Twitter.com/awarenessinc). Vice President of Marketing for Awareness, Mike Lewis (www.Twitter.com/bostonmike) knows that a large measure of success on social media is centered on how conversations get started and how deeply they engage the reader. Many companies see Twitter only as a broadcast or promotional platform. They successfully pump out whitepaper links, events, and products, but they are missing most of its power when they don't listen or engage.*

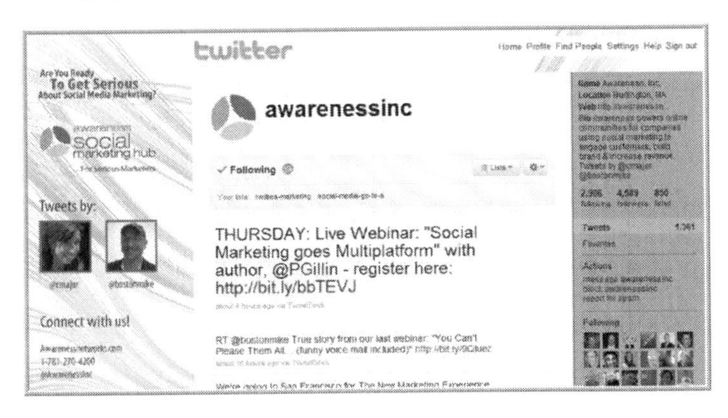

Mike and his team work hard to start conversations, engage their followers, respond and talk to others on Twitter. They have brought on thought leaders in various forms of social media to do webinars. To make sure that the material covered in the webinars is pertinent to their following, they often first use Twitter to elicit questions before and during live events. These live Q and A elements that Twitter facilitates have resulted in 10-20% increase in registrants, as events are happening. According to Mike, "Small business has to listen in order to grow their followers. They have to find key players, interact, and monitor for mentions of company name, common topics, the competition, etc. Participate! Engage! Get in and converse so you have something to actually measure."

While some elements of Twitter are not that easy to measure, in a more global sense, tracking them will help you create a bigger picture of your social media marketing presence and in some cases the impact. Some things to monitor are:

- Total membership of social media site
- Average number of total site page views per day.
- Number of friends/followers.
- Number of individual page views per day.

On a more individual basis, consider what your typical follower/friend is doing:

- Do they have a completed profile?
- Are they an inviter of friends/followers?
- Create and share on external list.
- Create and share on internal list.
- Of the friends/followers invited, what percentage accepts an invitation?
- How often do they log in?
- Do they join groups?
- Do they form new groups?
- Do they make referrals or connections between friends/followers?
- Are they contributors?
- Average length of post.

- Frequency of postings.
- Do they comment or leave trackbacks on other member's posts? Useful content?

There are some things to consider tracking while on Twitter. Think not just in terms of number of followers. Think in terms of categories of followers:

- New followers (member of Twitter less than 30 days).
- Followers 30-90 days.
- Followers over 90 days.

Then break those groups down further for analysis:

- Followers met online.
- Followers gained via business card.
- Followers gained via Facebook, LinkedIn, or other social media.
- Followers gained via email signature link.

From each of these groups, determine what business interactions you have with these followers. Is it business building, prospecting, or collaborative interactions? Things to review and monitor periodically:

- Collaborated with follower.
- Traded ideas/techniques with follower.
- Business related emails exchanged with follower.
- Referral gained from follower.

Are you overwhelmed yet? How the heck can all this information be aggregated and analyzed into usable data? There are some free tools for analyzing the basic information related to your Twitter follower.

Mr. Tweet: www.mrtweet.net shows who your influential friends in your network are. It also exposes who is following you, but who you are not currently following back and might have an impact on your network.

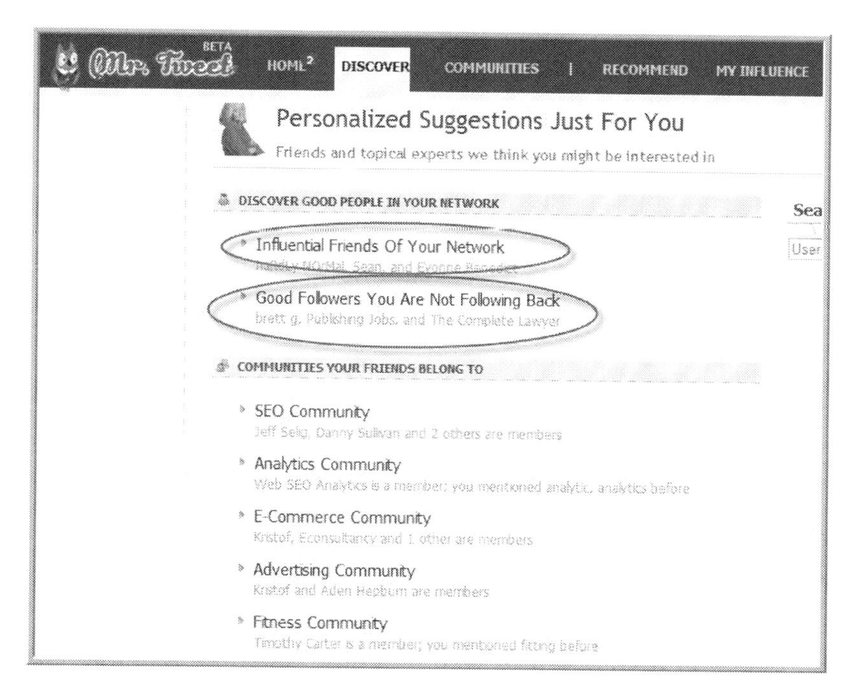

MR. TWEET RESULTS FOR @SHANNONEVANS

Click on "Good Followers You Are Not Following Back" to find lots of interesting people you may not have considered following, but probably should:

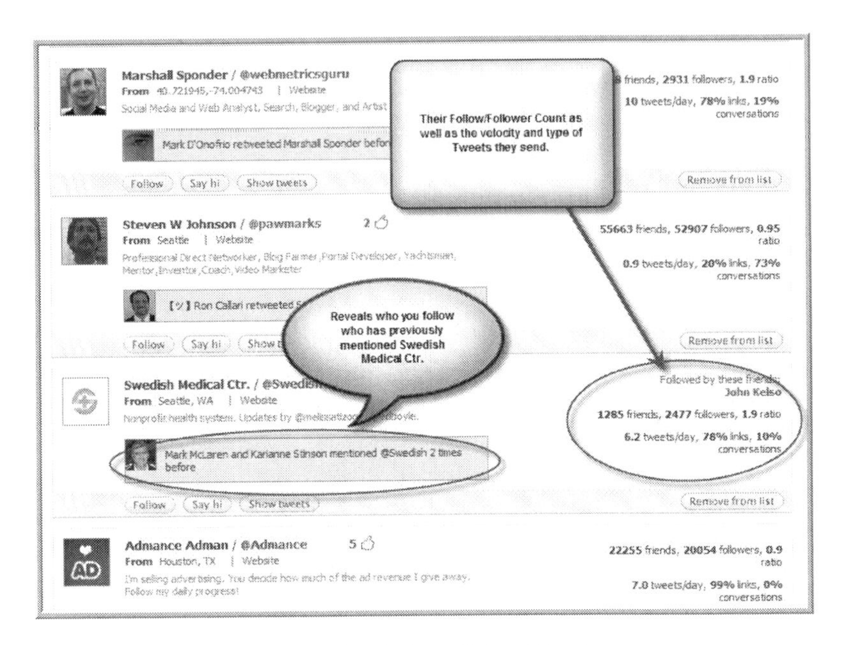

MR. TWEET DETAILED RESULTS PAGE

Qwitter: http://useqwitter.com is a free resource for identifying when you lose followers and after which post.

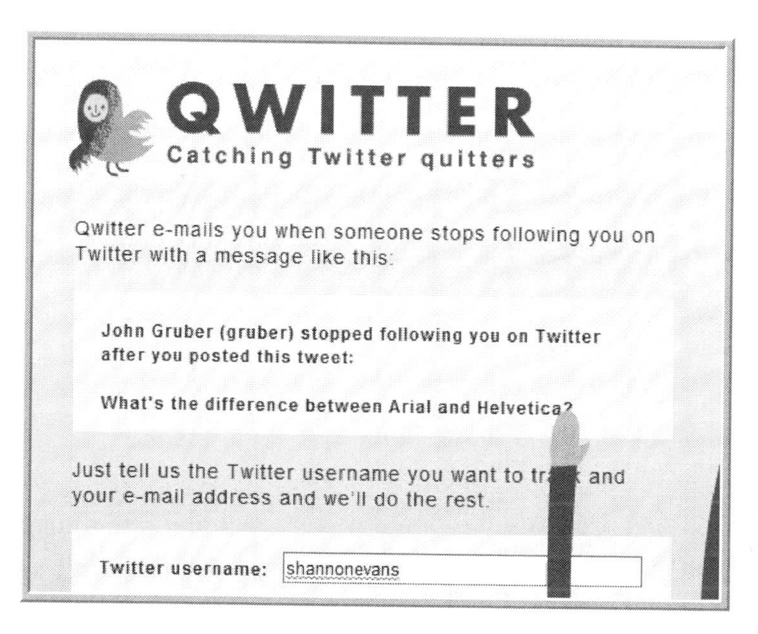

QWITTER HOME PAGE

Graph Edge (www.graphedge.com) is another useful tool for analytics regarding the followers you actually reach, the growth of your network, who unfollowed you, who are your most influential followers, and who your followers follow. It is a really low cost subscription based tool that costs less than a latte per month.

It is important in today's highly social 'real time' virtual world to know when your brand is talked about positively or negatively. For a coherent content strategy on Twitter, you need to track more than just brand mentions. In order to define, refine, and promote your brand, you first must know what conversations are already happening around your brand and between what parties, and what the general emotion/sentiment that is attached to those conversations. If there are problems to solve, questions to answers, or apologies and replacement parts to issue make it happen. To begin to analyze brand sentiment or topic related emotions/sentiment, there are some free, easy to use tools that analyze certain types of sentiment (in the form of keywords and emotional phrases) and return some useful information. However, they are not nearly as deep and actionable as more robust subscription tools. Thc following tools give you a rudimentary overview of sentiment around brand names, topics, and usernames on Twitter:

Tweetfeel: http://www.tweetfeel.com/ evaluates conversations on Twitter for positive and negative sentiment about popular brands, topics, and some hashtags. It does confuse sarcasm and slang incorrectly if there is no context clues. TweetfeelBiz is their fee based subscription analysis tool.

Tweet Sentiments: http://tweetsentiments.com/ evaluates Twitter conversations using NLP (Natural Language Processing) and Machine learning technologies to determine degrees of positive and negative sentiment related to a search.

Social Mention: http://socialmention.com/ works like Google Alerts, but searches in specific channels (blogs, microblogs, Facebook, etc) for any keywords you select to monitor.

Twendz: http://twendz.waggeneredstrom.com is an aggregating and sentiment analyzing tool for topics in dynamic 'real time'. There is an upgraded business version as well.

Trendrr: http://www.trendrr.com/ is a useful tool that tracks data qualitatively and quantitatively, examines sentiment, location, and trends as they happen and over time. It provides useful insights into topics and brand mentions. There is a scaled down free version, but the full blown version is quite pricey for small businesses.

Twittrratr: http://twitrratr.com/ examines the Twitter collective consciousness for positive and negative trends around a brand, product, person, or topic.

Case Example: *Lift9 is a company that does the data mining for their business clients when it comes to data mining social media accounts. According to Warren Sukernek, VP of Strategies, Lift9 came into existence because various agencies recognized that brand monitoring measurement of sentiment was important, but the tools were expensive and time consuming. The labor intensive analysis of the data extracted, often resulted in information that was not really that useful or actionable for their clients. It just was prohibitively expensive to get anything substantive for many clients. John Song, the founder and president of Lift9, decided to approach the problem differently. Song elected to create a research center in Vietnam. The people he hires are all highly trained process driven analysts and able to apply best practices to manually extract the data clients need. The Lift9 team dives deep to monitor, filter, and extract information from 8 different areas: blogs, Twitter, video, Facebook, forums, images, Wikis, and mainstream comments (and podcasts on occasion). Every post is manually graded for sentiment as the automated sentiment tools still have a long way to go. Warren emphasizes that they are analysts and do not engage with the client's audience, "It just would not be authentic for us to do that for them."*

Lift9 is focused on listening; because they look at data manually, they are able to extract more accurate data. Many of the automated tools are great for extracting number of mentions and indicating positive and negative language associations, though cannot determine connotation due to the limitations of the technology. "That is why our team is so successful," continued Warren. "We are adept at manually picking out the nuances which existing technology still has not been able to do as accurately." Lift9 is on the forefront of services that help companies listen, monitor, and measure their brands, so that they can create strategies to leverage social media like Twitter. Lift9 goes beyond the volumes and number of mentions by focusing on the 'so what' of social media, thus providing its clients with real, actionable insights.

**Note: Lift9 recently acquired Intrepid Research and Consulting (www.thinkintrepid.com).*

There are many more paid tools that can be useful if budget permits; however, if you are just getting started and on a shoestring budget, a little hard work and some simple tools may be all you need. Strategic services, like those provided by Lift9, are what help you make sense of the data extracted by the monitoring tools. Knowing what to do with the information you collect is what will set you apart from your competition. Is the information you monitor relevant and useful? What insights does the information gathered provide for decision making? What actionable information do you need? Look for value from the intended outcomes of your Twitter channel as you build relationships and work toward your business objectives. Keep in mind that tools give you data points, but only humans can provide insight. Just make sure whatever tools and processes you put in place are simple to use, scalable, and easy/affordable to sustain.

Marketing

Marketing professionals like Keri Mellott use Twitter to foster good public relations and personal relationships with businesses and consumers. They do this by checking @replies, searching for their keywords used by others, solving problems for themselves and others, answering questions, as well as promoting good people and events.

Steven Paul Matsumoto, CEO of Stigmare (www.Twitter.com/stigmare) and Emerald City Fashion Week (www.Twitter.com/ECFW) maintains an active social media presence and is an active blogger. He used Twitter to successfully re-launch his business after a significant name change in a down economy:

> *2008 was not a good time to be a highly leverage solo-preneur. I had been running my promotional products*

company Azimuth Branding with moderate success until about the middle of October, 2008. Ironically, September had been one of our best months on record. With everyone in a panic over the market correction that was starting many of my hot leads retracted and disappeared. I had been reading a lot about Twitter in Advertising Age and Media magazine so I invited my friend Eric Pratum out for drinks at the Columbia Tower Club in Seattle to get 'the skinny' on this microblog.

Prior to my chat with Eric, now with Spring Creek Group, I considered Twitter just glorified text messaging. As a matter of fact, to people that have never used it I find that is still the best way of describing it. The difference being I don't have to know you personally to get my message out. Eric convinced me of the value of at least venturing into Twitter. I of course started by following all the marketing and branding folks I could find on Twitter as this is why my passion lies. I began to have some great conversations and I began to develop a reputation as someone that 'got it' (whatever 'it' is) and began to accumulate followers rather quickly. This was late November and early December 2008. Then the snows came with one of the worst winters on record in the Pacific Northwest.

I had already been toying with the idea of re-branding my own company as my trade name Azimuth was in fuse by four other marketing firms globally and I did not want to run into Trademark litigation. Having always been a fan of Latin phrases I began searching out Latin words related to marketing to use as my company's new name. Surprisingly I came across the word Stigmare which is Latin for Brand. Even more surprising is that the url was available.

Stigmare, as a company name served two purposes for us: It spoke to what we do, something all too often forgotten when naming a company. It gave the firm an old world feel which was important as we had decided that our niche would be the luxury and lifestyle market. Over the last year I have positioned both myself and Stigmare as providers to and supporters of the fashion industry in Seattle.

It has been an interesting ride so far. I have made my fair share of mistakes. To many I am seen as a social media guy; but, I tell them it is just another medium to me. It's no different than a magazine article, televisions or radio ad to me. It is merely another way to communicate my message and make true, honest connections.

Steven Paul Matsumoto, CEO Stigmare, Inc. Couture Marketing and Product Development www.stigmare.com

If you are using Twitter to build connections and for customer relationship management (CRM), there are specific things to target to boost your company's reputation and overall brand loyalty. Increasing the quality and quantity of interactions with customers, suppliers and partners on Twitter is important for leveraging the power of Twitter.

Case Example: *Author-Clinician Noreen Wedman, uses a dual approach on Twitter. On her national account, www.Twitter.com/HealingToolKit:*

NOREEN WEDMAN'S NATIONALLY FOCUSED TWITTER ACCOUNT

She uses her national profile to build a professional reputation in the field of counseling in issues related to trauma and chronic verbal and emotional abuse. It is her hope to use this national Twitter platform to create a network of people, clinicians, and organizations that will benefit from awareness of her website http://mindbodyintegrativecounseling.com/ *and the next edition of her workbook Healing From Verbally Abusive Relationships. With her more local Twitter account www.Twitter.com/SeattleCounsel:*

NOREEN WEDMAN'S SEATTLE FOCUSED TWITTER ACCOUNT

Noreen is focusing on local Twitter users and often mentions local businesses that she frequents. The tweets are less formal and lighter in nature and often promote her private practice and local support/advocacy groups.

Twitter is a powerful tool for establishing a rapid feedback loop which can result in boosting a company's reputation and increasing overall brand loyalty. You can leverage Twitter to meet the needs of your company through increased sales, improved customer satisfaction, and through the immediacy of access.

Chapter 11: Twitter And Local Customers

Twitter now has location based API (application programming interface) that allows you to filter your followers by location. This means Twitter has the capability of increasing your local impact. Twitter Local is a tool that allows you to search using geographically specific search parameters. It has RSS (Really Simple Syndication) feed capability that gives you a powerful way to monitor all kinds of local feeds.

You can first search for local Twitter users by using the search feature:

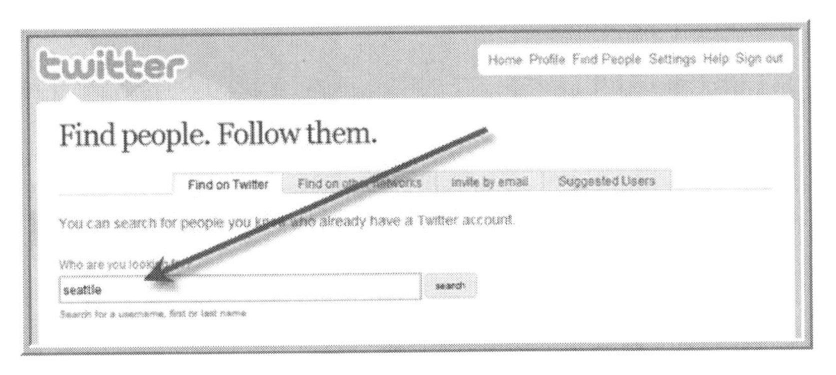

LOOK FOR LOCAL TWITTER ACCOUNTS TO FOLLOW

Follow the locals that you think are influencers or actively participating on Twitter:

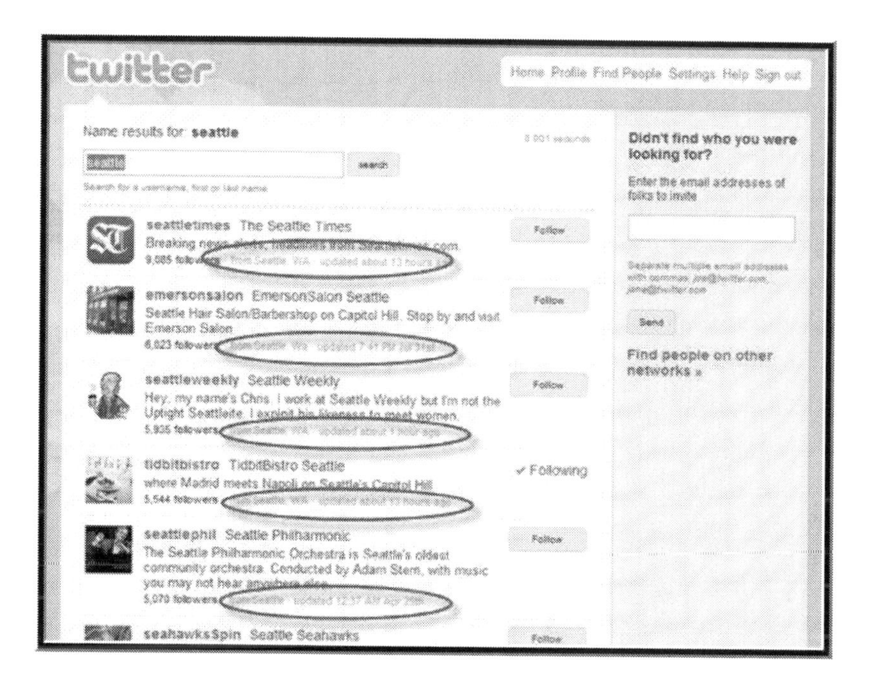

RECENT TWITTER MESSAGES FROM SEATTLE ACCOUNTS

You can direct message them (DM) with specialized local messages to encourage more local Twitter account owners to follow you. Make it personal, specific to your location and your customers. Do something unique like offer a special discount on your product or services for mentioning Twitter, give them a survey to answer, ask for their feedback on something. Whatever you do, make sure that you look and act local.

Twitter discussion threads and popular hashtags show up in Google results and Bingtweets.com. Businesses with use Google alerts to search for and follow mentions of their name. Tracking these mentions is useful for observing what consumers are saying and to find ways to improve user experience. It can be used to increase your user base and to examine your market share in order to better understand who is talking about you. Encouraging and engaging them in a dialogue increases the search engine generated traffic as well.

Using Twitter Local

Twitter has great local search potential. It is a great tool for building a cost effective PR and marketing program. It attracts local clientele and allows you to announce important events and get immediate feedback, reviews, and reactions from your current customers. Twitter is the social pulse of a large sector of today's buying public. Consider how Twitter provided real time information in the case of public events in Mumbai and in Iran. You can easily see the power of those 140 characters.

To maximize the local impact of Twitter for your business you must think local and concentrate on promoting things that promote your local community.

Tip: The benefits of using Twitter are growing almost as rapidly as its membership. Some of the most powerful benefits of Twitter are:

- Send clients/customers individualized messages.
- Create personalized messages targeted at your specific audience.
- Take the "pulse" of your customer base regarding new products, services, ideas, etc.

If you want to have primarily a local presence, consider adding a local element to your Twitter name. Here are some easily identified Seattle/Tacoma Twitter accounts:

@Tacoma_News

@Seattleweather

@Huskystadium

@TheRealMariners

@oaklandreviews

@tacotimepnw

@kayjayfm

If you want to test the power of Twitter locally, find who is tweeting near you.

Let's say that you are a restaurant in Chicago. "Restaurants" is the largest local search term. Try testing it in the Twitter search bar using "*Chicago Restaurants*".

Look at all the conversations associated with that search phrase:

By having a local search "tag" in your listing, you can create and encourage local search traffic and conversation about your business. You want customers to talk about you on Twitter:

"I just ate tacos @ sancarlos with @localsearchsea yummy!"

There are several ways to search for users by location, Twitter search for PC's and Twitterfox.com for mobiles are just two. To search for local Tweeters to follow, use one of these applications to search by city, community name, etc. To get locals to follow you back, offer them incentives like "kids eat free – 1 per adult" or offer a special Twitter discount if they say today's special on Twitter.

Once you have established your Twitter persona, you will want to cultivate your local presence by connecting with others in your community. Search for other local Twitter users by searching for them by city name, user location, etc. You can then begin to follow and respond to local search queries with a direct message.

For those who elect to send and receive tweets via their cell phones, local search shows which service type businesses are tweeting about their specials. The great thing about SMS tweeting is that not only does the message show up on the screen, but the phone number does too!

Who is tweeting near you? Twitter local is a great tool that lets you search user geo-targets. You can use the RSS feed (found on the right hand side with the little orange box on Twitter beneath the search bar) to monitor Tweeters locally. Try a search on Twitter that is geo-targeted: "Restaurant Seattle". Restaurant is the most frequently used local search term.

> ***Tip***: Some local search Twitter applications to investigate are:
>
> www.chirpcity.com
>
> www.Twitter.com/advancedsearch
>
> www.nearbytweets.com
>
> www.tweepz.com
>
> Even if you do not plan to post or tweet yet, capture Twitter account names relevant to your business. There is no cost to obtain a Twitter account (or more than one) and it makes sense to own it before this technique becomes more popular.

You can even use traditional local search techniques for promotional purposes on the Twitter stream. Promote events, listings, and classified type ads carefully so as to not "over promote" and looking like you are direct selling. Instead, consider infusing local ratings, reviews, educational content, and community service announcements by using geo-targeted language integrated into the social stream of consciousness discussions and proclamations on Twitter.

As Twitter becomes more popular, you may gain additional business from using Twitter above and beyond just the boost in local search results. In the following example, you will see how a Papa Murphy's Pizza store in Knoxville TN is using Twitter to promote their store (with a plug for the NCAA Basketball tournament as well).

This screen shot is from early April 2009 and they really don't have that many followers. However, over time this could easily change dramatically and this local store might rank higher than other larger chains.

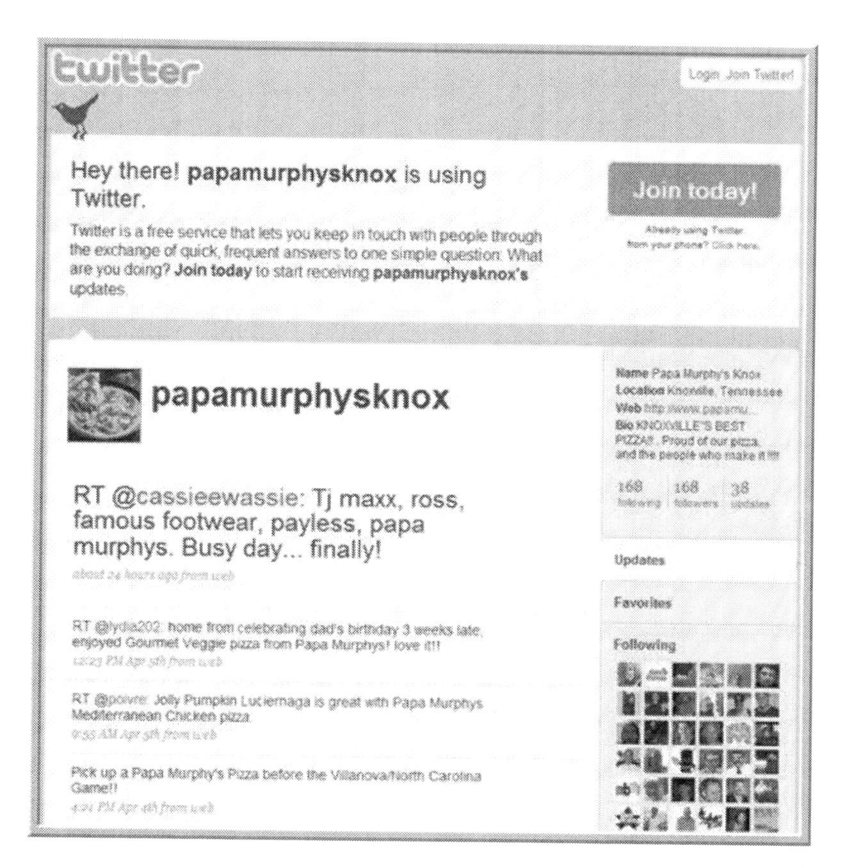

PAPA MURPHY'S KNOXVILLE, TN TWITTER ACCOUNT

If you are a brick and mortar business or an online business with a local presence, consider selecting a Twitter account name with a local flavor.

For example, if you are a dentist in Bellevue, WA why not snag the Twitter name "Bellevue Dentist". Your profile will have your real name and URL, as well as a brief description that you provide, so there is nothing potentially stopping you from using the power of local search in your Twitter moniker.

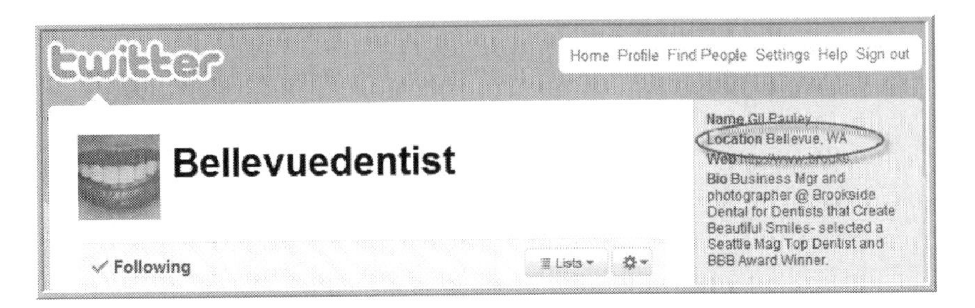

USING A SPECIFIC LOCATION IN SEATTLE METRO AREA

How can a business use local search to their advantage on Twitter? First, create and publish a professional looking Twitter page so people can communicate with you. Include a link to your business website in your profile. Perhaps use your logo or a photo of your store front as your avatar (profile picture) so people will come to recognize you by sight. Then get people talking about you.

Let's say your restaurant is the Salty Dawg Diner in Seattle. Your Twitter name on your profile could be "saltydawgdiner." Your patrons can promote you on Twitter with messages like,

> *"I just ate fish and chips @saltydawgdiner with @localsearchsea!"*

Offer a special discount to patrons who will tweet from the table for the server on their iPhones. Ivar's (a popular seafood restaurant) in Seattle did this recently to celebrate their founder's birthday:

> Happy 104th Ivar! Mon 3/23 get special. Buy entree, get 2nd for $1.04. 3/23 only. Say "Happy b-day Ivar" 2 get it.
> http://tinyurl.com/d92rsb
> *1:10 PM Mar 20th from web*

Really creative businesses can combine traditional local search with their current discussions by intertwining it in the conversation. If it is a listing, event, or even a classified type listing with a little imagination you can work it in easily. For instance, you could create a post like: "New cameras with polarized lenses on sale tomorrow @SeattleCamera."

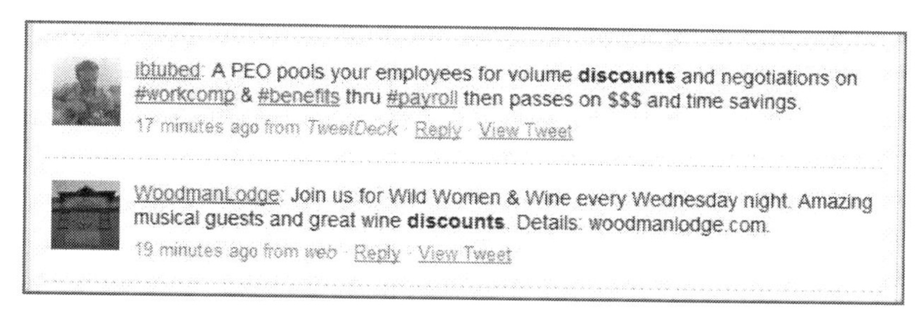

Try something with a little more creative edge to garner local reviews, ratings, anything that can be geographically targeted.

> *"Saw new play @MillCityPierTheatre with @shannonevans and was impressed." Or, "The ice @skateoutsideSeattle is perfect tonight."*

To take advantage of local Twitterers' regional expertise, you will need to court them. Follow them and send them special direct messages (DM) thanking them for their follow backs. Make your interaction with them through @replies and DMs. Keep your tweets conversational and personalized to these local customers.

Talk to your customers and tell them useful information that helps them keep you in mind as their local choice. Ivar's in Seattle does this to perfection in their tweets:

> @Andersonimes Either Acres of Clams or Salmon House are great. +Both have awesome Happy Hour from 3:00ish 2 close, 7 days/week. KEEPCLAM
> *10:26 PM Apr 18th from web in reply to Andersonimes*

Cultivating your local presence on Twitter helps you not only to build brand reputation, but to also build Google search engine results. Twitter related Google listings can result when you tweet with locally targeted messages.

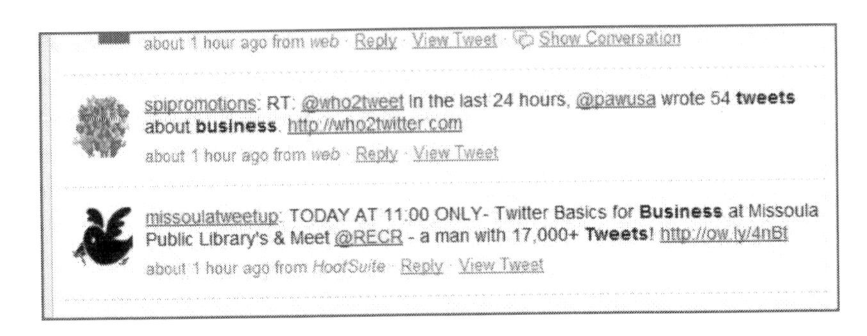

When you embed geo-targets (location names) in some of your messages, it increases traffic generated by local search and when you have more traffic, you increase your user base and ultimately your market share. It creates a better user experience for your community when they can relate to your messages.

Help your business use Twitter effectively to attract local business. Treat your customers with respect and ask for their advice and opinions about your goods and services. Acknowledge your customers as individuals and use them to check your company's social pulse. You will reach individual communities with your unique message that is personalized for that audience. Share useful information and ask for community involvement; your company's local presence will expand exponentially.

Chapter 12: Twitter and Your Business

Traditional marketing has historically used outbound, interruptive push marketing tactics; the nature of the delivery systems that were available for marketing dictated that they be that way. Telemarketing, direct mail, email, print, TV, and Radio are all good methods for getting your company and your products 'out there.' The overriding problem today, with only using traditional marketing avenues to build brand recognition and to market your goods and services, is that it does not deliver your message in a targeted enough method. It is the shotgun blast method for shooting and hoping you hit your target audience.

Inbound marketing is the highly targeted and more exact "rifle shot" method of marketing. Inbound marketing audiences are generally warm and receptive to your message and your brand because it is permission based marketing. These people have signed up to be "in" your circle and to hear what you have to say and share. Those who signed up for your blog feed have had to request the RSS. To join your Facebook fan page or to get your tweets, they had to purposely select a button to "be a fan" or to "follow." To find on your website/blog, they had to actively search for you by topic or by site name. It is not random that they follow you in the first place. They had to plug some permission-based language in somewhere to get to you.

Case Example: *Suzanne Evans, marketing guru (www.Twitter.com/SuzanneEvans) and owner of Help More People (http://www.helpmorepeople.com) joined Twitter in December of 2008. She was really resistant to joining at first, but people in her inner circle convinced her to try it and see what it might do for her business.*

Suzanne is a dynamically effervescent people person. She was not initially keen on Twitter because she loves to engage with individuals and felt she might find a better more personal venue in other social forums. After a little arm twisting, she dug in with her usual 'full steam ahead can do' attitude and discovered that 'this Twitter thing really works!'

Suzanne found that Twitter gave her a larger public forum to meet people and grow her professional following. Her first adventures into Twitter were a huge success in attracting more potential clients, as it literally helped to increase her exposure to a wider audience which helped to explode her business.

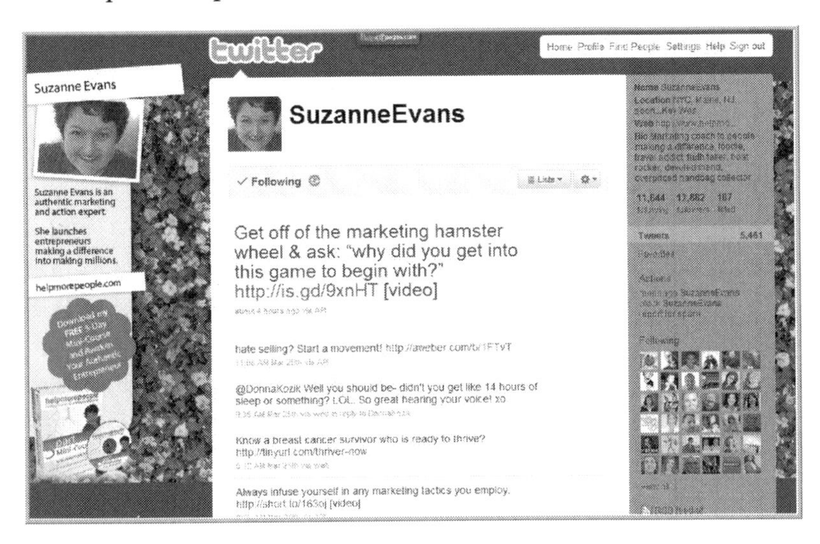

She gained about 1000 followers in the first few months on Twitter and worked to grow her following organically without the use of any automation tools. She now has more than 12,000 followers. Not bad for a former Twitter nay-sayer!

Suzanne launched a few new programs for her business and began to talk about them in conversations on her Twitter account with some of her followers and with people she was following. In less than 90 days, Twitter was directly responsible for an additional $13,000 in income! Suzanne was amazed, "A known entity on Twitter started talking with me and then tweeted some glowing recommendations about me. So those people who knew and trusted *her began to follow me and it just exploded! It was a marketing 'AHA!' moment that was life changing."*

With Twitter, Suzanne has been able to reach more followers with her Help More People movement. She wants to help people make a difference and Twitter has been instrumental in getting her message out to an ever growing audience in an affordable, rapid delivery system.

How Twitter Benefits Your Business

You have to walk a thin line with your followers when you begin to monetize Twitter. Even when you do that small bit of self-promotion, you want your tweets to be informative and interesting so you keep your followers reading. A good rule of thumb is for every 10 tweets you post; send only one self promotional tweet. Don't inundate your followers with advertisements. Even your marketing messages should be interesting and informative. If you avoid blatant advertising, you will get more click-thru's and more sales.

> ***Tip***: Here are some more ideas for business to use to get started with Twitter:
>
> Restaurant: announce daily special, new chef, change in menu, upcoming holiday events or early closings.
>
> Realtor: new listing, change in interest rates, open houses, etc.
>
> Chamber of Commerce: local events, monthly luncheon, featured member, calendar.
>
> Travel Agent: special fares, discounted packages, new laws that impact foreign travel.
>
> Bookstore: featured authors, sales, book signings.

For the sake of example in the service industry, a dentist's office is used to illustrate how Twitter can be used in broadcasting, lead generation, marketing, and audience engagement. This plan could apply to doctors, attorneys, health clubs, physical therapists, chiropractors, hair stylists, massage therapists, estheticians, etc.

When you walk into most dentist offices there is usually a rather generous waiting room with back issues of Redbook, Readers Digest, and People Magazine. Imagine instead there were two laptops near the front desk, open to the clinic's Twitter account and the homepage of their website? People who are already on Twitter might be inclined to add the clinic to their own account on their mobile device or when they get back to their computer at work/home. The clinic would of course reciprocate and "follow" their clients.

People who have immediate access to Twitter in the clinic will be inclined to immediately leave a comment about the service they get or how great they feel after their visit. It encourages your clients to get involved in social media and responding about goods and services. It provides them with a place to provide specific feedback as well.

Not every company has the time or the money to create and maintain a good blog. Twitter is a good cost-effective alternative blog. It is smaller, less time consuming and requires smaller bits of information, the payoff can be quite similar to that of a blog.

Case Example: *Ravi Sinha, CEO of Track2Media, a communications consulting company, needed to help a company in transition due to a recessionary market and an internal shift of leadership. Turtle Animations hired Track2Media to help reposition their brand in the market as a credible organization worth funding. Track2Media made Twitter a large part of their social media toolkit to generate curiosity among funding agencies about Turtle Animations. As a result of Track2Media's intense efforts for their client, Turtle Animations is back on track, winning awards and designing some sizable animation projects.*

If your company does not blog either on your website or on Twitter, you are missing out on a rich opportunity to stay in touch with clients and vendors. You are ignoring a huge segment of the population who you could attract with name recognition to your brand. You are also missing out on an easy to implement reputation management tool. When you have a strong online presence, it is easy to monitor and track your pervasiveness in the market place.

Case Example: *Jane Mackay, author and editor for Janemac Editing (www.Twitter.comjane_mackay, www.janemac.net), lives in Sonoma County, CA. She uses Twitter for branding and client attraction:*

> *"On professional discussion lists I had read two colleagues' tales of success in attracting clients through their Twitter usage, but had thought that their experience must be outside the norm. So, when I asked a new client how he had found out about my service and he replied that he had linked through to my business website from my Twitter profile, I was both surprised and thrilled.*
>
> *It turned out that I had primarily received this honor by dint of being the first person to follow him when he created his Twitter account, which rather dashed my hopes that it was erudite and oft witty tweets that had made me think, 'This is the editor I want for my book!' But that's fine; I'll take luck as a matchmaker.*
>
> *Luck of course plays a large part in so much of life, both professional and personal, but preparation and integrity lay the foundation for that luck to strike. I know that my tweets reflect on me as a professional, as an editor, and as a person. (As does my website, which is why I put a great deal of thought and research into its desig and creation.)*
>
> *I am not a consistent tweeter; life and, yes, business, often get in the way. But I do try to check in at least a few times a week, if only to post my "Word of the Day" and see what's new with some of the writers, fellow editors and other interesting people I have come to feel that I know. My hope is that over time Twitter will become a standard part of my business promotion, at the same time it is a medium for connecting with others. And, always, a fascinating glimpse into human life and nature."*

Perhaps the biggest argument for implementing Twitter is that because it is permission-based marketing to begin with, you are attracting and not chasing clients. Twitter is a great SEO tool to help you track conversations for particular keywords and topics. It is incredibly useful for spotting trends as they unfold. It is also great for finding those who are influential thought leaders. Find who are the thought leaders, who is talking about your keywords, and who your industry, follow and engage them.

Once you figure out who is talking about your brand, your industry or your keywords, you need to know what to do with that information. How do you collect it and what do you do with it? How will you categorize it? What use is that information to you? Will you use Twitter as a data collection mechanism or will you use it for PR? Or will you use it to build a giant digital community for customer relations, crowd sourcing, and lead generation?

Case Example: *Joe Hage, (www.cardiacscience.com) Director of Marketing Communications at Cardiac Science, manages their Twitter account. Joe received a tweet from a tweeting paramedic Tom Bouthillet (www.Twitter.com/tbouthillet) inviting @cardiacscience to check out a blog post.*

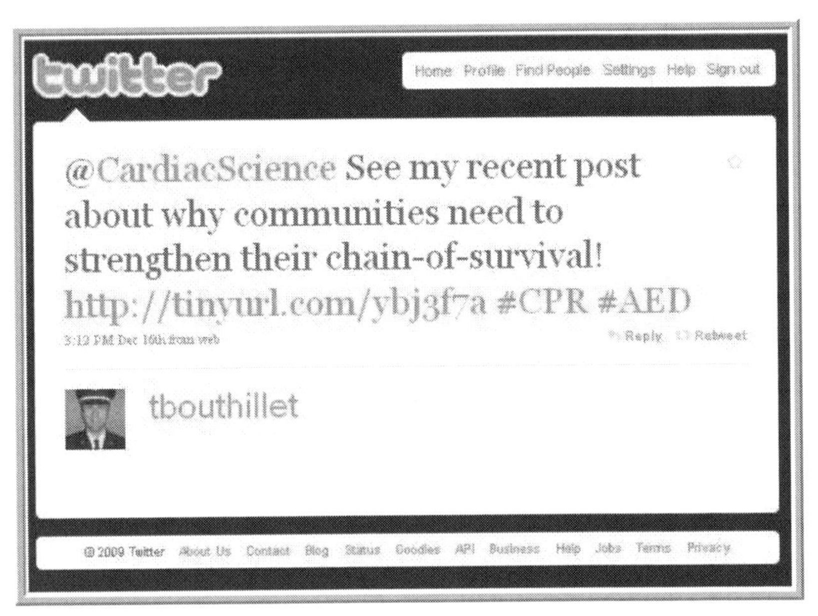

The overall content of the blog was excellent. Tom and Joe then connected over the phone and discussed Tom creating a guest post on the Cardiac Science blog. As a subject matter expert, paramedic medical device consultant, and Tom's passion for educating the public about life saving techniques and technologies, Tom is able to reach people in a way that Cardiac Science can't. Tom's voice is invaluable because his reach is far different than that of a corporate entity in a hyper-regulated industry.

Joe watches carefully for mentions of his company name, their products, or any mentions of groups and organizations that need their products. It has led to many interesting interactions on Twitter:

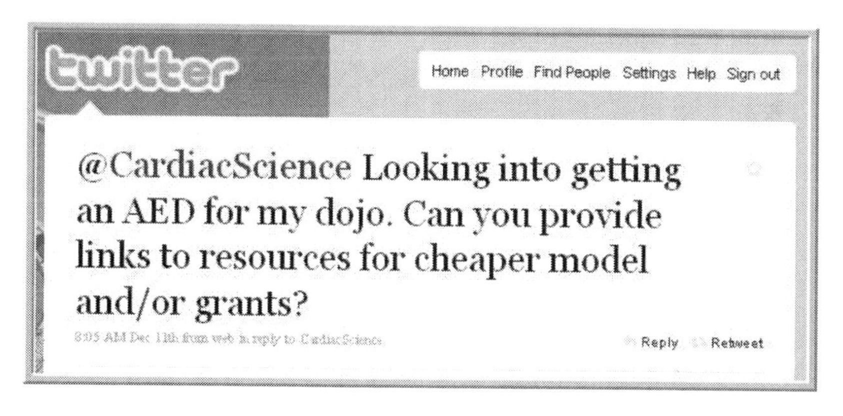

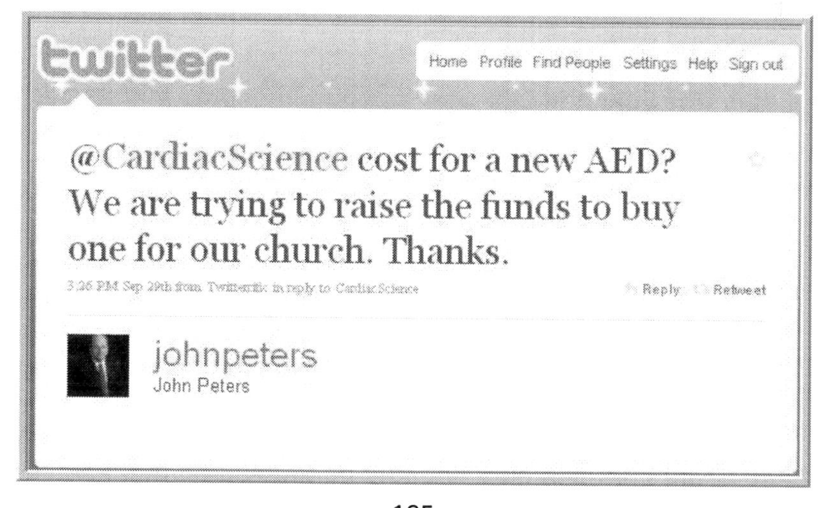

The marketing of defibrillators and ECG medical devices may not be a high profile group on Twitter, according to Joe, "The lesson to be learned here is that regardless of your business focus, there will be people who are 'into it'. They will follow you if you are active and you engage with them."

Tip: No matter how you use decide to integrate Twitter in your business keep in mind these simple rules:

- It is not all about you or your product/goods/services.
- No one cares about features...they only want to know how it benefits them.
- No selling, instead of selling lead the world to your goods/services/products.
- You have to be a friend to have a friend.

Chapter 13: Twitter and Sales

If you do use Twitter for sales and promotions make sure you are providing useful information to your target audience and that you or your staff are ready to engage with them. The following are some ways that other businesses have used their Twitter account for sales and promotion.

Promotion Coupon:

Borders Extended through Memorial Day! 40% off one item in stores & at Borders.com with this **coupon** >http://ht.ly/1RLKX
about 12 hours ago via HootSuite

Sales Effort:

MacCools Come to "Foothill Village Side Walk **Sale**" Thursday, July 29 at 11:00 am until
Saturday, July 31 at 11:00 pm.... http://bit.ly/an2G2k

Twitter exclusive rewards:

isyaias Check out this week's **Exclusive** #Travel Deals for our @CheapOair **Twitter** followers! spon http://tinyurl.com/2bvelgp
about 1 hour ago via web

Featured item or service:

Rob Wills, owner-operator of Redekleen Commercial and Residential Carpet Cleaning of Everett, WA has begun to use Twitter to enhance his company's chances of ranking with search engines. They use Twitter to promote specials, share information about environmental hazards in the home, etc.

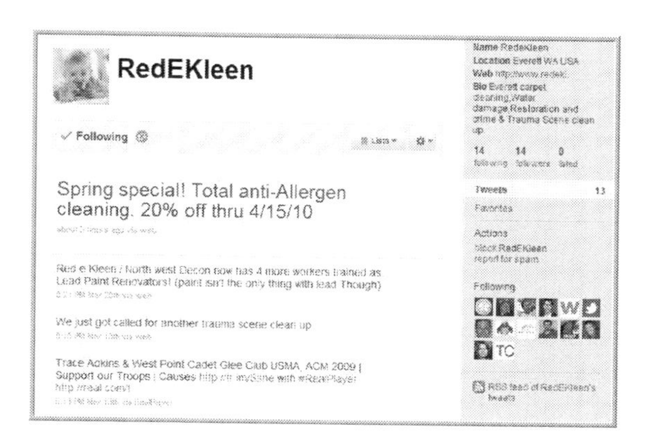

Putting your brand name out there for the world to see, opens you up for contact with the world at large. Make sure you connect with your customers through solid, useful information and links that increase the click-thru rate for your website. Pay close attention to your direct messages. Answer questions, and connect with the people who take the time to contact you personally so you avoid the perception of spamming.

Case Example: *Barbara Reininger, owner of* www.MyKidsCookies.com *and www.Twitter.com/MyKidsCookies understands the value of Twitter for her small business.*

Every box of cookies she ships includes a business card that says "Follow me on Twitter". Barb sends out tweets every few days about what's baking, specials, community activities on Bainbridge Island, and fun things about cookies. Valuable informative or useful Tweets provide positive exposure for your company.

Twitter as an Inbound Marketing Tool

Three things are needed for lead generation in any business – initial contact, conversion, and analysis. In today's Internet business world, companies spend a lot of time and money on SEO (search engine optimization), blogging, article and press release writing, and on Social Media Marketing to make their business/brand "findable". Businesses then focus their efforts on converting their visitors, once they "find" them. The savvy business owner today has landing pages that are "sticky" and capture the potential client's contact information in exchange for a free offer of a white paper, ebook, podcast, etc. This is all used as part of the businesses' lead tracking intelligence and lead management tactics. Really sharp business owners then analyze the information to create an edge over their competitors.

How do you go about getting inbound marketing traffic from Twitter? What are the processes and tools businesses can use to work to convert followers into customers? Inbound marketing processes are standard marketing tactics:

- Get Found
- Publish
- Promote
- Optimize
- Convert to Customer
- Test
- Target
- Nurture

Getting found on the Internet is a little different than traditional marketing methods. You must publish good, useful information, promote judiciously, and optimize the heck out of it all. Converting your audience into paying customers requires testing, highly targeted material, and the patience to nurture and develop relationships with the "listening" audience.

Case Example: *T-Mobile is an international company that struggles with their multiple identities on Twitter. They are a well known brand with typical customer service issues. Fairly early on, they created Twitter accounts in the U.K. and in the U.S. The U.K. was fairly straightforward with their Twitter strategies. Unfortunately, the U.S. account(s) have not really been clear on the techniques and strategies that are effective on Twitter.*

tmobilenews
TMobile | United States
Account Created, everything looking great so far. So, when should I start spilling the beans?
9:08 AM May 2nd, 2009

tmobile9797
tmobile blackburn
Slow Sunday 6 months ago

tmobile7393
Tmobile Santa Monica
Hey guys, our BOGO deak has been extended to June 20th!! So come on in and check out are cool new handsets and plans. 4th & wilshire 6 days ago

TMobileLex
TMobile Lexington | Lexington, KY
Buy one, Get one on all smart phones! Stop in to get your new smart phone today! *some restrictions apply. See store for details 11:51 AM May 6th

tmobiletest1
Tmobile USA
Do you have electronics on your Christmas list? Best Buy is giving away $1000 gift cards for today only! http://wholeurl.com/bestbuygc 5 months ago

TMobile_Test1
@TMobile_Test2 I was thinking we could just chill.
3 months ago

TMobile_Test2
@TMobile_Test1 Hey Bro, wanna tweet together bro?
3 months ago

There are dozens of accounts which are poorly defined, poorly managed, and many apparently abandoned. With a simple audit, it is difficult to tell if some of the accounts are official or if they are contracted. The naming conventions and nomenclature on the various accounts is inconsistent. Even worse, customers and potential customers are posting questions to the accounts and getting no response. As a result, some have gone out on Twitter and other social media platforms and complained, perhaps justifiably, that T-Mobile's customer service is lacking.

To get found by your potential audience, you must first find the street corners where they "hanging out" and "talk". In Twitter, you only need to go to the search feature and enter your brand or your keywords to find out who is talking. Create good content for your website, blog, and social media sites that promote who and what you are. As you produce content that is keyword rich and focused on your niche so that you begin to be seen as an authority figure on the Internet. If you also have a highly optimized website, your tweets and your website will work together to generate real inbound links that will be measurable and productive.

Create product buzz and then let your followers tell your story to their circle of "friends":

- Get others talking about you. Don't just toot your own horn.
- Be memorable! Engage your followers. Avoid boring repetitive information.
- Give details, provide pertinent facts, and how to do things.
- Use words - not just links, meaningless tweets, or lingo.
- Be brief, be concise.

Keep in mind, the modern consumer is jaded. They want immediate gratification in answers to their questions. If they find you pushy or irrelevant they will dump you. Be interesting, be available, and be remarkable.

Case Example: *Warren Sukernek, President of Social Media Breakfast Seattle, was on his way to Anaheim, CA and planning to stay at a large national hotel chain's facility. He checked to see if they were on Twitter and saw that not only did they have an account, but they were tweeting a discounted rate for the time he would be there.*

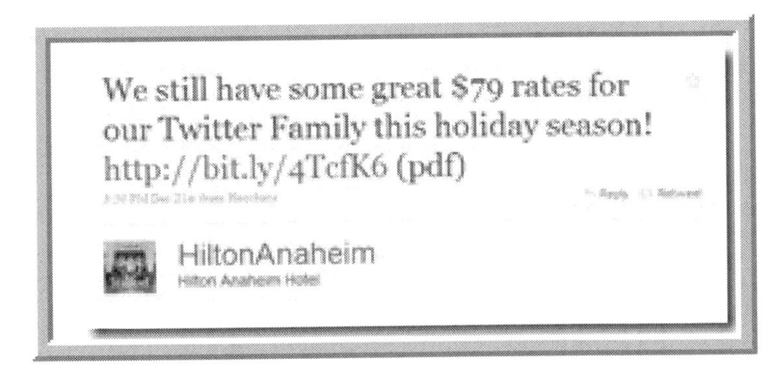

TWEET SENT FROM @HILTONANAHEIM

To show his gratitude, he followed them and tweeted to his rather large following about his upcoming trip and the hotel.

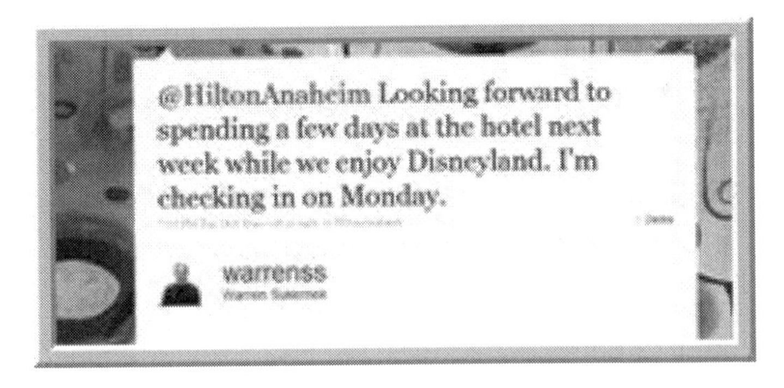

WARREN'S DIRECT RESPONSE TO @HILTONANAHEIM

There was no response from the hotel's Twitter account. He then tweeted while actually staying at the hotel about being there.

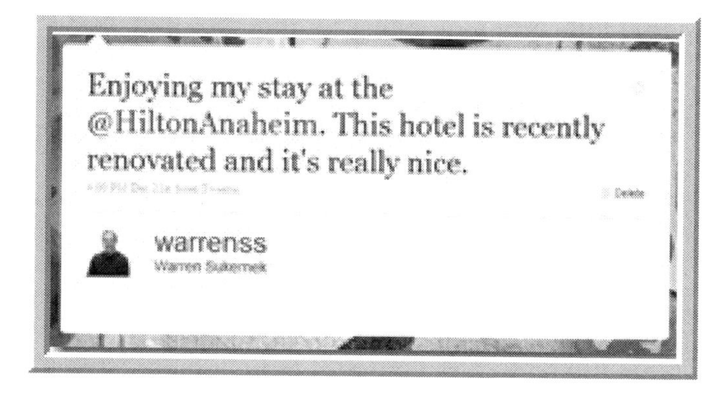

WARRE'S NEXT ATTEMPT TO CONNECT WITH @HILTONANAHEIM

No response. Warren then went to the hotel's Twitter account and looked at it more closely.

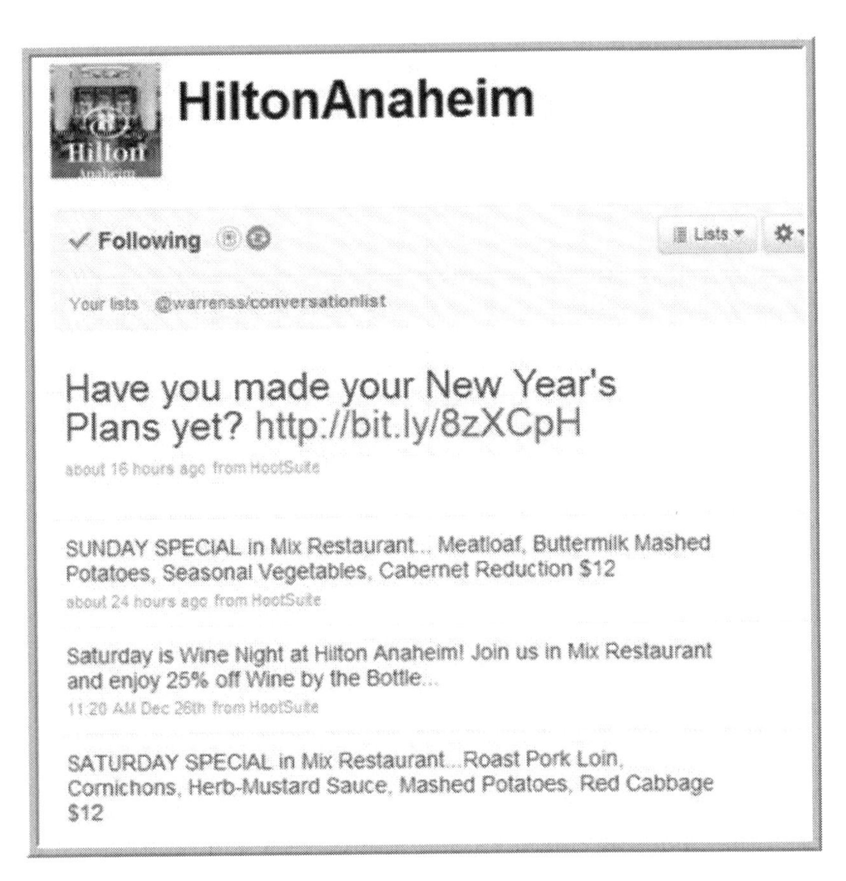

@HILTONANAHEIM'S TWITTERSTREAM FOR THE SAME DAY

At that time, the Twitter account was all broadcast and no interaction. This prompted Warren to write a blog post on ttp://Twittermaven.blogspot.com about his experience and about hotels that 'get' how to use social media. There was STILL no response from the Hilton Anaheim; however, there was a groundswell on Twitter from other Twitter users who follow Warren. Finally, a week later Hilton Anaheim responded by Tweet and by email. But by then it was too late. As Warren puts it so aptly in his December 2009 blog post, "The glass is half full for the Hilton Anaheim, you can advertise your specials on Twitter or you can engage with guests to turn them into evangelists."

Social media has such low barriers for entry and as a result, many companies don't try to understand customs, expectations, etc. Instead, they push and broadcast, and end up alienating rather than engaging with people. The relationship of people (in your network) to you and your product, as well as the interactions and insights the business gains from those followers is incredibly valuable to building business presence. The ease with which Tweets are received both on PC's and on mobile phones makes it increasingly attractive to businesses. It is a quick and easy way to access a captive audience to gather or transmit information to customers or to build brand presence.

Customer Relations: customer service is a significant factor in any business' success. Twitter offers a great way to reach out and enhance communication with your customers.

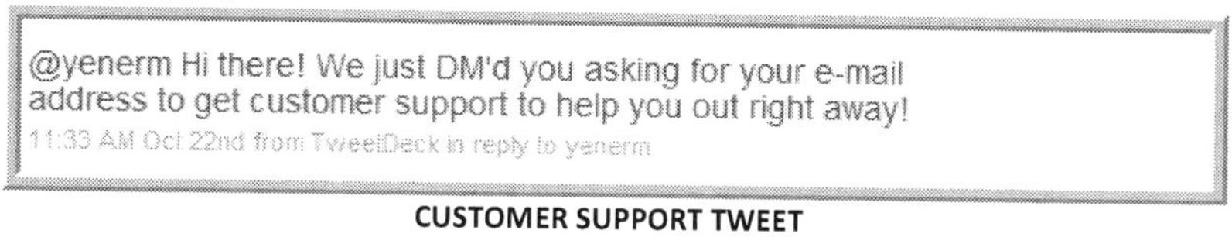

@yenerm Hi there! We just DM'd you asking for your e-mail address to get customer support to help you out right away!
11:33 AM Oct 22nd from TweetDeck in reply to yenerm

CUSTOMER SUPPORT TWEET

Case Example: *Leaming Chee-Brown, co-owner of Reiki Fur Babies (www.Twitter.com/reikifurbabies), already had a website, she blogged, and* ***then*** *she registered for Twitter based on her brother's recommendation. She had no clue what to do after she signed up. She asked her brother, "Now I am in there...what do I do?" His answer, "just talk! You are really good at that so just be you but on Twitter!" Ming began to talk about her passions, Reiki and animals. She added a photo of her dog to her background and the results were amazing!*

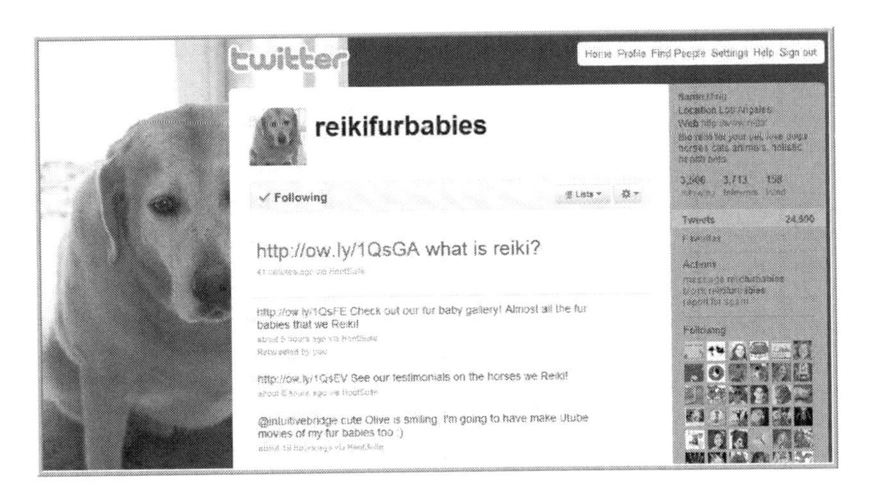

@REIKIFURBABIES TWITTER HOME PAGE

People were immediately attracted to her page and began to interact. Ming began to interact with people from all over the world including such places as Wales, Dubai, Texas, Finland, etc. Having a unique place to post comments and photos led potential clients to her website; it has enabled her to reach a worldwide audience and to more rapidly connect with others and establish trust.

While Reiki Fur Babies uses their Twitter account to promote events, specials, and talk about their success stories, they also use Twitter to create synergy with other Reiki practitioners. Twitter has become a terrific platform for educating the public on what the power of Reiki both for animals, and their owners. Education is the key to expanding their customer base, and according to Ming, it is working far better than they ever expected! Now, she is so afraid of missing an opportunity to communicate with a potential or existing client that she has her DM's go straight to her Blackberry so she can respond immediately.

Monitoring the Twitter stream provides an inexpensive, online communication solution for questions, concerns, and complaints. No more phones ringing at all hours, no more "push nine for" recorded messages. Now you can respond online in real time as the need arises.

Solicit Feedback: Before the Internet existed, businesses had to spend large amounts of money on focus groups to get valuable feedback. Feedback tools are now virtually free with social networks like Twitter, creating virtual conference rooms filled with people clamoring to take a survey.

SURVEY LINKS IN TWITTER

It is also a good place to post links to survey results and ultimately, guide followers to useful, pertinent information related to your goods, products, services, or niche.

LINK TO SURVEY RESULTS

Product Development: Twitter is a great place to share opportunities, technology, and development cycles. Twitter provides a platform for rapid inclusion of customer feedback into the development of products.

MaximSchram Cover story: Unilever to use social media to aid **product development** | News | New Media Age: http://bit.ly/ctUDsz
about 12 hours ago from web

@dreisiebzig Games, study/productivity tools, and entertainment apps are all on deck for the Livescribe App Store. Stay tuned!
10:50 AM Oct 22nd from TweetDeck in reply to dreisiebzig

Brand Building: one skillfully fashioned tweet can have a great impact on your following, to not only guide viewers to your site, but to also raise brand awareness and promote valuable content on your website or blog to your niche following. Brand building through promotions:

TeleNav Just 6 more days to enter our #7Words Contest for the chance to win an Apple iPad! #KO http://su.pr/8TThPa
less than 20 seconds ago via web

PROMOTIONAL TWEETS

Lead Generation: Twitter is a useful tool for getting leads in various ways. One good way to get leads is by asking questions about other's goods and services or to listen to the Twitter stream for anyone else asking questions about specific products, goods or services related to your market. For example, suppose you work for an educational consulting agency for school districts with a large at risk populations. You could start a Twitter conversation with the schools conversing about their problems with students and procedures, or you could do some data mining from their bios and see if you can figure out how to contact them directly.

Perhaps, you are a company that sells blood pressure cuffs to home users in your local community. The following tweet is an example how you can create an opening to talk to someone who is using medication for blood pressure issues and inform them about how to find the information they seek.

TWITTER USER ASKING FOR INFORMATION

Case Example: *Through conversation and some cultivation, they will become aware of your products and services. Matt Heinz (www.Twitter.com/HeinzMarketing) of Heinz Marketing has clients who use a combination of Twitter and shortened traceable URL links (like bud.url or bit.ly) to track lead generation and registration offers to attract potential prospects.*

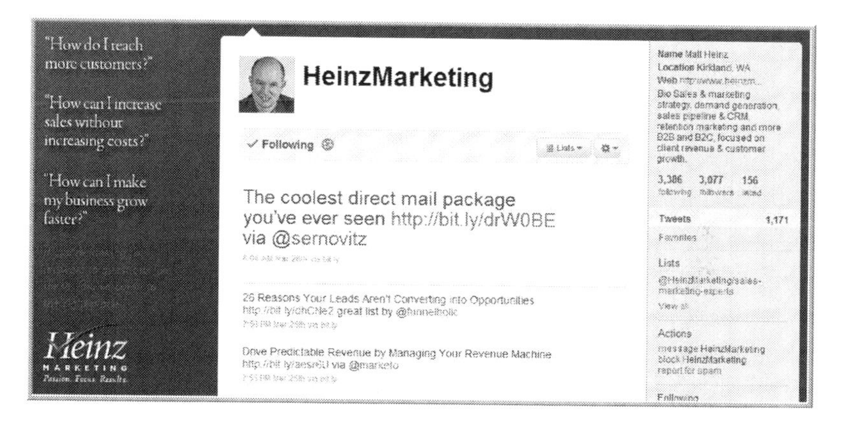

HEINZ MARKETING TWITTER PAGE

Initially, the volume started small but Heinz has seen an increase as the number of targeted followers grows. As they continue to tweet, high value content that is intended to inform their audience, Heinz's clients quickly gained credibility and trust with their audience.

Scouring Twitter for contacts and potential leads is only limited by your time and imagination. Realtors, Insurance agents, carpenters, restaurants, etc., with a bit of data mining effort, can make Twitter a worthwhile place for lead generation. Who is your ideal client? Can you provide them with solutions to their immediate problems? Do you know how to communicate what you have that brings benefit to them clearly and tangibly? Can you devote the time to monitor and return tweets with your target audience?

Related URLs: you can use Twitter to lead readers back to your blog or company website for useful information for your niche audience.

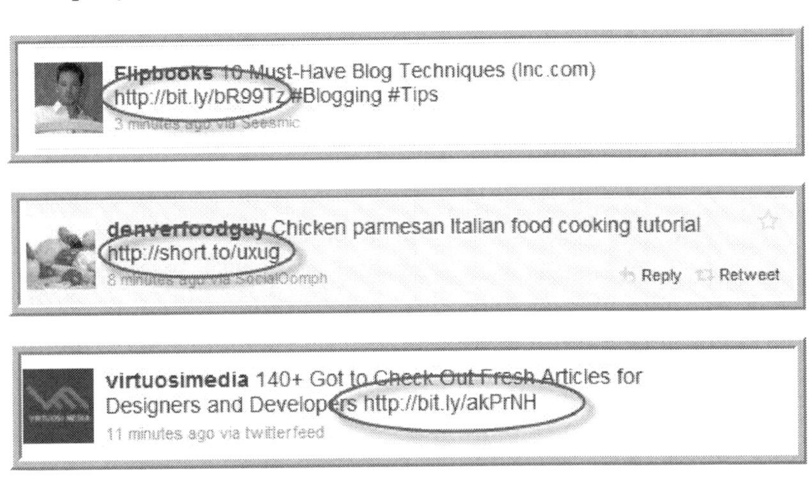

LINKS LEAD TO RELATED INFORMATION

New Product Announcement: use Twitter to launch a new product, website, blog, or service. It creates an instant channel for spreading the word!

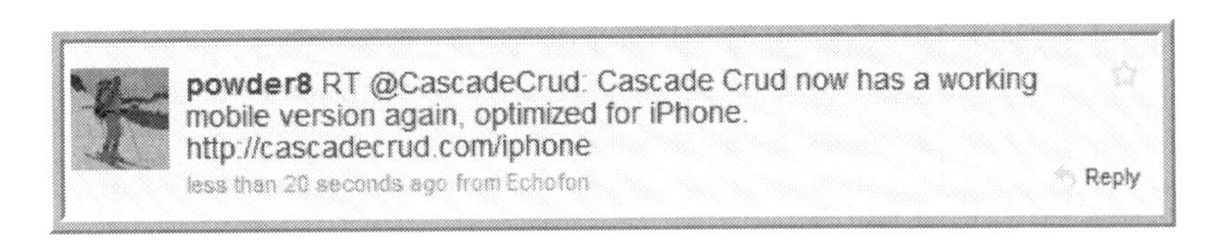

pc_deal A **new product** Veriton M420 has been added on Aroxo http://pcs.aroxo.com/7Mlu
8 minutes ago from API

jayhawknj RT @footpetals: Foot Petals is introducing an all **new product**, Sporty Soles! Watch for the Fit and Fabulous 411 and RT to win a pair http://bit.ly/afw3AC
35 minutes ago from TweetDeck

USE TWITTER TO ANNOUNCE NEW PRODUCT ANNOUNCEMENTS

Latest Press Release: A sizeable following on Twitter, this is a great way to release news (fee-free), in addition to standard distribution channels for press releases. More and more journalists, bloggers, and reporters are turning to Twitter for news ideas.

nicksipc Published a new post: Maryland Lobbyists Ranked By Compensation - www.citybizlist.com (**press release**) http://tinyurl.com/yg46msg
1 minute ago from Ping.fm

ELICOMPUTERGUY LSI Announces Advanced Software Options for MegaRAID 6Gb/s SAS/SATA Adapters - PR Newswire (**press release**) (http://cli.gs/5dqRL)
half a minute ago from WP to Twitter Reply Retweet

PRESS RELEASE LINKS

Testimonials: product testimonials are powerful. If you get new testimonials on your site, why not draw attention to them!

My_Ipad_News Ipad: The iPad: Terrible Name, **Great Product** - Picket http://bit.ly/cK5nma
11 minutes ago from Twitter Tools

Pastor_Paul Dear @Telstra staff at Griffith Shop rocks**!! Thanks for **great** service!!Na!!These guys really know the **product** & explain patiently(-!

26 minutes ago from web

CUSTOMER REVIEWS

But also watch for negative reviews that provide an opportunity for response and to address customer issues.

Events: Twitter is the perfect venue for event promotion, product launches or special occasions.

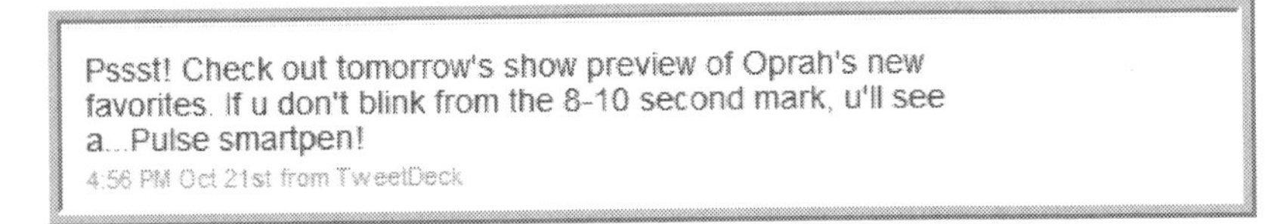

Posting links to sign-up pages are highly effective for increasing event attendance and raising awareness:

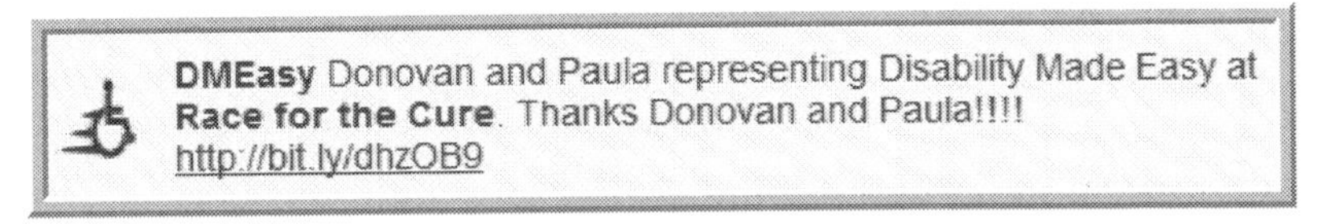

Case Example: *Social media marketing guru Matthew Mikulsky, owner of Chatter Creative Design Firm (www.Twitter.com/ChatterCreative and www.chattercreative.com), uses Twitter every day now. At first though, Matt was originally a HUGE naysayer, as he only saw Twitter as "just another time suck social playground that was a constant tickertape of information and*

news." But his print marketing clients kept saying that they wanted to use Twitter and needed him to show them how to use it effectively. Matt decided that regardless of how "spazzy" the tool was, he would have to figure it out and see if it had any business potential for his clients and customers. Taking that leap literally changed how Chatter Creative did business.

CHATTER CREATIVE'S TWITTER PAGE

Matt attributes a lot of his recent success on using Twitter as an icebreaker, "Previous to using Twitter I never could get past the gatekeeper at some companies. Now I just cultivate a relationship on Twitter first and I have a way to get my foot in the door!"

Since much of Matt's work at Chatter Creative is visual, he has found Twitter a great resource for getting instant free feedback from other professional 'creatives'.

@IdeasUnfold the difference between RGB & CMYK & Pantone? It's a colorful world we walk! #printing #design
4:05 PM May 19th via HootSuite in reply to ideasUnfold

Twitter is definitely changing the way people do business. Matt's tweets emphasize good content, positive language, and useful information. His attention to this 'spazzy' tool has really helped his content get wide exposure. According to Matt, "Good listening skills are important but so is having an eye and an ear for good content. That's the key to success on Twitter."

Good content can rapidly become viral on Twitter and other social networking sites. Typically new information, videos, and blog posts from authority sites go viral faster than most other content. Rarely does product information or hard selling Tweets go viral. Posting good niche-related blogs, videos, and podcasts are always relevant. Sharing photos from events and presentations that are pertinent are good too. Product related news is also useful.

If you are short on material to post, consider using www.google.com/blogsearch to search for blogs related to your niche, for ideas and material to share with your followers. Get in the habit of listening to what is going on around you and you will become "tuned in" to finding good material to share with your audience. By becoming established as an authority in your niche, you will encourage your followers to make the all important click thru to your website.

The webpage perspective followers first see when they finally click thru is where conversion happens. How do you get them to stay once they get there? What irresistible offer do you have that makes them stay and "poke around?"

A good landing page is critical. It should have a way for the first time visitor to opt in for additional information, a special offer, a video, a podcast...something that makes the visitor eager to part with their email address. There has to be a call to action somewhere on that page. Their email addresses are precious as they provide an excellent analytic for lead intelligence.

No links + No referrals = No leads

To make all this work, you have to use the right language so your audience knows what to do on Twitter, your site, and any other place you lead them. Humans are inherently lazy and unless you give a compelling reason and specific directions, most will never make the effort to discover that the material you are sharing with them is useful, exciting, or important. Tell them what they need to do using specific, actionable verbs. The power of suggestion really does work!

Case Example: *Calvin Lee, owner of Mayhem Studios of Los Angeles, California started his Twitter account just to 'test the waters' for his business. He started first with small talk on his account, www.Twitter.com/mayhemstudios, and it suddenly snowballed into something bigger. He used no programs, no automation to grow his account into more than 44,000 followers. He just uses Twitter to have conversations and talk with people. Today, he continues in that vein, remains friendly and open in sharing information about design related links, Photoshop hints and helps, and information for business owners on marketing and branding. Calvin has shared more than 83,000 conversational and informative tweets with his followers.*

Calvin has found that Twitter has created a great venue for connecting with people before a networking event to 'hang out' and get to know each other. It helps to break the ice and makes the actual event more effective for networking because the people feel like they know you a little and have something in common: Twitter.

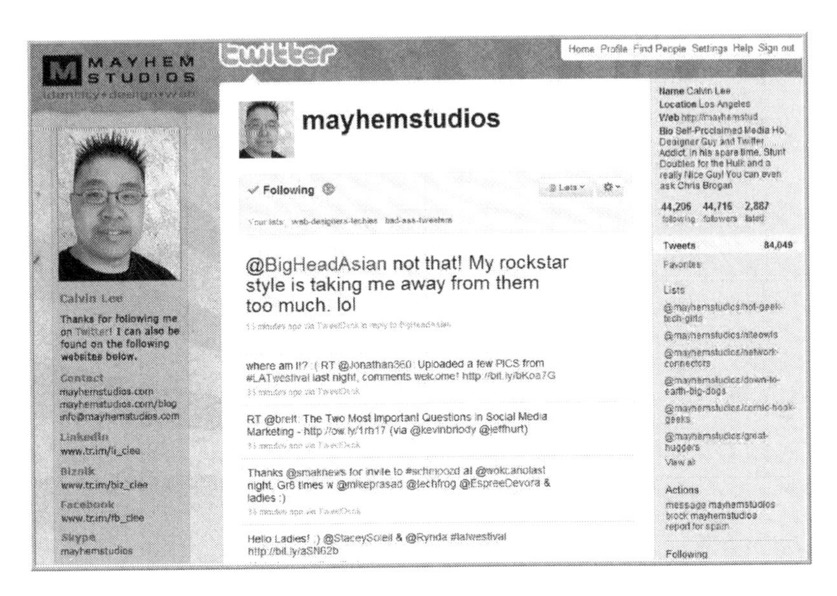

CALVIN LEE'S PROFESSIONAL TWITTER IMAGE FOR @MAYHEMSTUDIOS

According to Calvin, "My followers have followers and that makes for a HUGE ripple effect. I find that if someone asks me a question then I better know what I am talking about when I answer! The interaction between people on Twitter is amazing. I love being able to talk to people who have been to my blog where I am talking about my latest project or the business of design who then come to Twitter to talk. It really lets me get an immediate pulse of the people in marketing and those trying to find good marketing and design firms. That is too cool!" It is easy to share in Calvin's enthusiasm about Twitter as a conversation and marketing tool.

At the end of the day, micro-blogging can be what sets you apart from the rest of the market. People buy from those they trust and those who are confident in their knowledge. Marketing does not have to be salesy, sleasey or pushy. Authentic marketing is about checking in and referring good information that helps your readers.

Tips: Here are some action verbs to consider (by no means is this a comprehensive list) using:

- View, link, share, comment
- Play, stop, watch, embed, link, share
- Read, post, share, examine, add to cart
- Link, tag, rate
- Buy, tag, review

Social Web Analytics and Some Really Cool Tools

Using analytic tools are useful for general reputation management and basic sentiment tracking. The analytic tools you choose should enable you to formulate a plan for who you want to follow, allow you to create an 'indexable' database worth using, and let you extract data from the web to analyze and make into a usable collection of information.

How often do you focus on marketing? How do you measure the effectiveness of your efforts? Create time in your schedule each day or each week to devote to marketing your business on social media. It is "doable" if you have the right tools in place to help you manage that marketing requirement. Planning, consistency and focus will help you wrap your head around the process you have to go through to make online social media marketing work for your company. Use a step-by-step method that builds one upon the other. Just like any other thing you do in life, if you have the right tools you can make this work for you and help you get more clients and customers.

Here are a few of the tools that are easy to implement, that let you focus your marketing message, help you find your ideal clients, what they are talking about, and most importantly find where they are "hanging out"!

Hoot Suite: A free dashboard tool that allows you to manage multiple profiles in one master account. (CoTweet is a similar app).

Tweetdeck: Another free dashboard application that allows you to cross post to Facebook. It has various columns that you can customize for direct messages, groups, keywords, etc.

Twellow: Twitter's version of the Yellow Pages.

Twinbox: Allows you to feed your Twitter feeds into your Microsoft Outlook.

Twitterhawk: Marketing tool that lets you monitor Twitter for users who are talking about keywords and phrases you select.

Twitter(ur)ly: Allows you to follow popular brands, trends, products, and topics on Twitter.

Cligs: An app that allows you to find what visitors are saying about you and your brand.

Tweetie: iPhone app to use for Twitter messaging.

Tweetgrid: Allows you to track a keyword or phrase.

GroupTweet: Lets you privately message on Twitter to a designated group. It is an internal instant messaging system.

Twitoria: A neat little tool that allows you to clean out inactive tweeters in your following.

Monitter: Lets you follow local Tweeters who are talking about what you are interested in knowing...your brand, your name, your keywords, your products

Bubble Tweet: Interface tool that lets you post videos on your Twitter profile.

Twit Pics: Allows you to post links to photos in your tweet stream.

Tweepler: A tool for sorting your followers and help you decide who to follow and who to ignore.

TwitThis: A button (piece of code) you can add to your website or blog that lets visitors post a Twitter message about your content.

StockTwits: See what traders and investors are tweeting.

HelloTXT: Lets you update your status across all social media platforms simultaneously.

TwitterFox: Another dialog dashboard.

Future Tweets: Allows you to schedule future tweets.

Twtqpon: Allows you to create exclusive coupons to post in your tweetstream.

Tweetburner: URL shortener.

Tweetbeep: Hourly tracking of conversations that mention you, your products, your company, etc.

Twitter Counter: Allows you to compare your Twitter account to others.

Twitter Safe: Allows you to back up your list of followers.

TrackThis: Track UPS, USPS, and FedEx updates to you Twitter Direct Messages. Lets you know when your package changes location.

Twhirl: An application that runs multiple social media accounts simultaneously (Twitter, Facebook, etc.).

Splitweet: Web based application that allows users to manage multiple corporate Twitter accounts from one platform. It alerts you when others tweet about your brand.

Retweetest: History of individual retweets.

Tweetmeme: Lets you place a TweetMeme retweet button ion your website and blog, so your audience can easily tweet your content on Twitter.

Tweetlists: Most popular links tweeted over last 24 hours.

Twitlinks: Tech talk.

Tweetfunnel: A tool that allows companies to approve and schedule the tweets they post.

Tweetscan: Alerts you when your selected keywords (phrases) are mentioned on Twitter.

Tip: Consider using Twitter to:

- Create a coupon campaign.
- Stimulate viral marketing efforts.
- Provide customer service.
- Establish focus groups.
- Manage customer expectations.
- Select vendors.
- Resolve conflict.
- Recruit employees.
- Generate traffic to your website.
- Build brand fervor.

The list of resources continues to grow daily as new developers put out new apps and new tools become available. The best part of this rapid growth is that people can choose based on their personal and professional preferences and unique needs. There is bound to be an interface out there that works for you!

Why use Twitter apps programs? Because they are searchable! Search.Twitter.com allows you to gather information and monitor the latest URLs pertinent to your site, your brand, and your clients. Apps make it really easy to peruse your unique history quickly and easily. All the messages are preserved and that saves you time. Use Twitter to monitor your brand, and to do some other creative things that will attract more customers to you and your goods and services.

Chapter 14: Twitter For Non-profits And Government Agencies

Non-profits have a unique selling position on Twitter. It is a valuable tool for getting others to share your good work, share the work of other non-profits and to further a good cause. So what can a non-profit do to raise awareness of their purpose, their issues, and to raise money for their organization?

Twitter is a great way to extend conversations with your donors and with potential donors. The successful Twitter non-profits are the ones who listen carefully. Use Twilert, a "Twitter alert" application, to set up regular alerts related to your brand name, products, services, special interests, keywords and phrases, or even when a particular person posts a new tweet. This app makes it easy to follow your organization's name, your cause, or your top contributors, so you can read and directly respond to them, and to promote more active awareness and engagement with your cause.

Twitter is a useful tool for cross-promoting your blog because it allows you to link valuable posts to stimulate conversation and awareness. It is also a great tool for promoting your contributors. You can acknowledge their gifts publicly and immediately, as well as mention their business or their website. It is also an inexpensive and effective way to promote your event. You can provide links to registration for your fundraisers and events; you can post announcements and event summaries, and announce important breaking news.

To grow your Twitter following, you want to have a clear idea of what you are focused on and who you want to attract. Then go out and find like-minded people using keyword searches on http://www.search.Twitter.com or other Twitter search applications.

Promote them, post links to your website, share stories and experiences...get out and engage in an on-line conversation. Know and perhaps even follow those who respond to you. Add your Twitter ID to all your social profiles and to your email signature. Your following will grow and awareness of your non-profit will grow at the same time.

From a fundraising perspective, you can use Twitter to engage donors (and potential donors), create and maintain relationships, meet people around the world who are interested in your cause, and promote traffic to your website. It is a powerful tool for listening in on conversations around the globe on what people think and have to say about issues related to your non-profit's focus. It is a great way to get real-time advice as well as to get a conversation started. What a powerful listening post Twitter can be a powerful listening post to hear what others have to say about issues that impact your mission!

Twittering about your non-profit does not guarantee that people will flock to your event or instantly whip out their check books and donate. It is a tool that raises awareness, build relationships, and drives traffic to your website. It is but another tool to help people and organizations communicate and build rapport. People give to organizations they can identify with and trust.

Start today on Twitter by searching for terms like “fund raising”, “non-profit”, or “charitable organizations”. Look for your cause, join in on the conversation. Start telling your non-profit’s story. See who's talking and follow those you find interesting. Once you do, you will learn more about the people who support your cause, and they in turn will teach you to be more effective in telling the story of your non-profit.

If your non-profit has a staff or an active advisory board, have them each create a slightly different version of your non-profit's Twitter account. Let them talk from their own perspective and begin to connect to more and more people. Cross promote to your organization's fan page on Facebook. Link to your organization's agenda, calendar, announcements, blog posts, etc.

One of the most powerful things you can use Twitter for with non-profits, is the ability to have a back channel for people who are attending your fundraising event to rave about what is happening in real time. Create a unique hashtag for each event. This often results in additional fund raising from their friends and followers. It creates almost a competitive carnival environment for the attendees to get caught up in the enthusiasm of the moment.

Case Example: *The Puget Sound Blood Center has an active Twitter account (www.Twitter.com/BloodCenter) that is used to draw awareness to the Twitter community of immediate, emergency, and on-going needs for blood supplies in Western Washington. They also use their local platform to encourage more blood donations, nd to answer questions, discuss eligibility, promote donation events, and to communicate with donor volunteers. Sean Debutts (www.Twitter.com/seandebutts), coordinator for the Blood Center's social media relations, also uses Twitter to cross promote their Facebook Fan Page, where donors can directly schedule an appointment to give blood. Sean also uses Twitter to promote individual Facebook donation team pages, where different organizations create a competitive event to encourage and promote blood donations.*

OFFICIAL TWITTER PAGE FOR PUGET SOUND BLOOD CENTER

They post at least twice per day and as a result, have seen an increase in donations each month. Ninety percent of their tweets are oriented toward other Twitterers and less than 10% are donation request oriented. They use their stream to promote events, inform/educate the public, and to promote other non-profits.

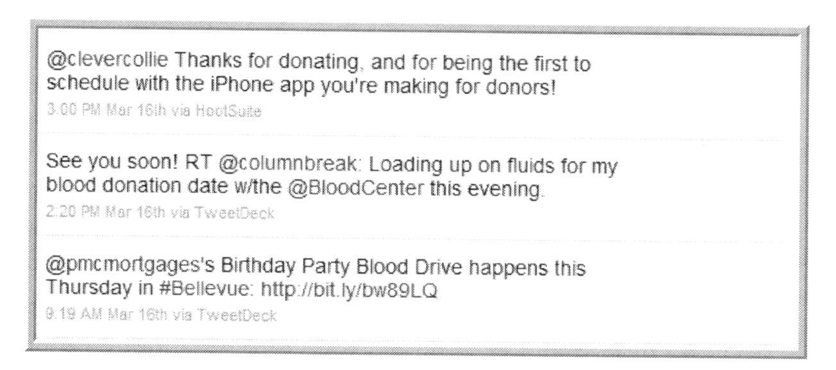

Sean has been amazed at how Twitter has become a great community to meet other non-profits and exchange ideas, as well as to cross promote each others' events. He has worked hard to make the www.Twitter.com/Bloodcenter account fun and competitive, and to remain consistent with the Puget Sound Blood Center's message.

Their goal with their Twitter account is to build real-world relationships that increase donations, and to get the word out in emergency blood shortages.

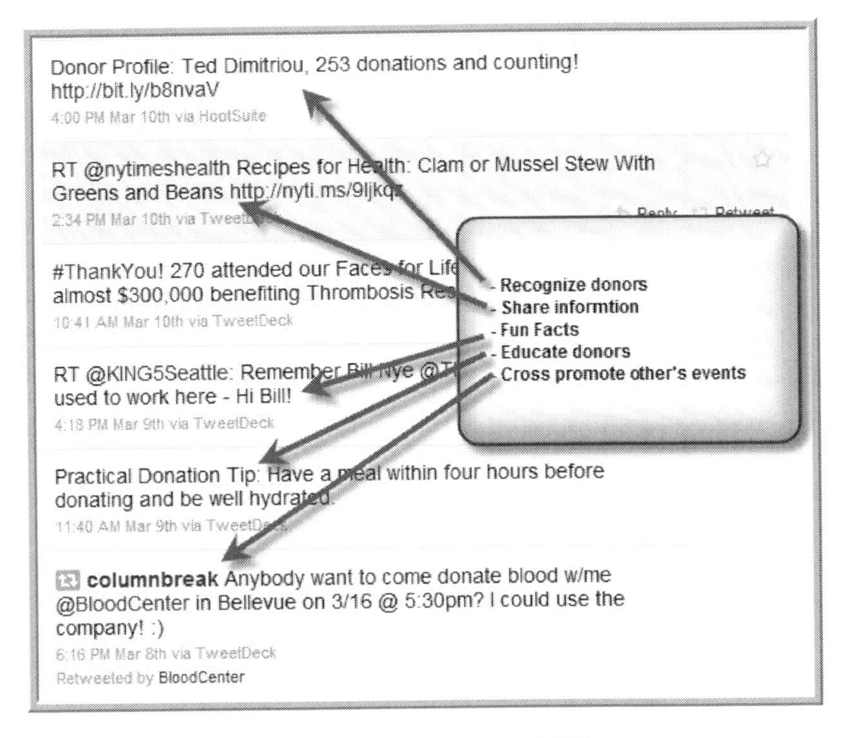

ACTIVELY ENGAGES WITH FOLLOWERS

Twitter for non-profits is a cost effective (FREE) way to promote who you are and what you do. It is an additional, but powerful platform for getting your message out quickly, spreading your message, and raising awareness for your cause.

Government Agencies Using Twitter

Local, state, and federal agencies are using Twitter and other social networking platforms to raise awareness and share information. The Obama campaign organization did this well, and his administration continues to share information from various agencies including offices like the Government Accounting Office. The GAO uses Twitter to keep the American people informed of their efforts and to share informational videos they post on YouTube.

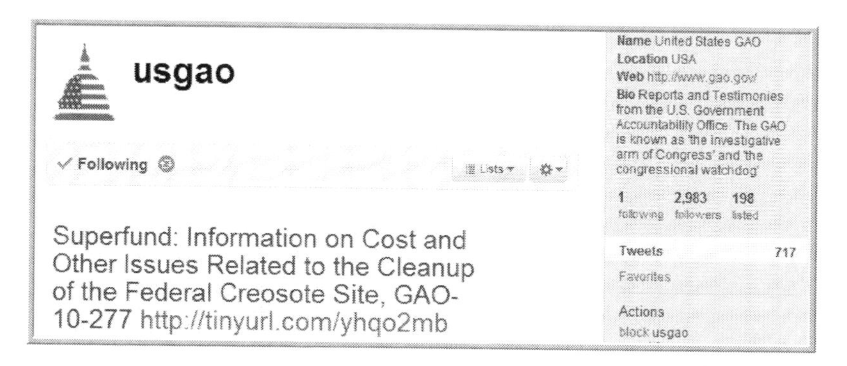

US GOVERNMENT ACCOUNTING OFFICE'S OFFICIAL TWITTER ACCOUNT

Twitter is an ideal tool for public safety and emergency notification. The Los Angeles Fire Department uses its main account @LAFD to post bulletins about fires, injuries, etc.

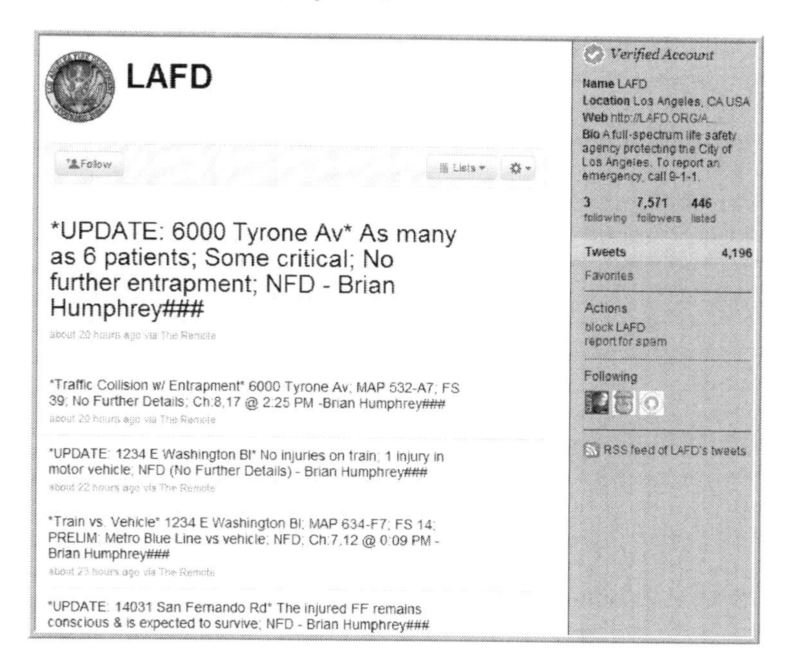

When a commuter train derailed in 2008 in Chatsworth, C.A., resulting in multiple fatalities and hundreds of injuries, LAFD tweeted updates. LAFD also tweets during wildfire seasons to update the public and responders on wind direction, evacuations, and hot spots. They use their @LAFDtalk profile for more interactive tweeting.

There are many police and sheriffs' departments that use Twitter to report crimes and ask for public assistance in solving cold cases. Others use it for traffic reports:

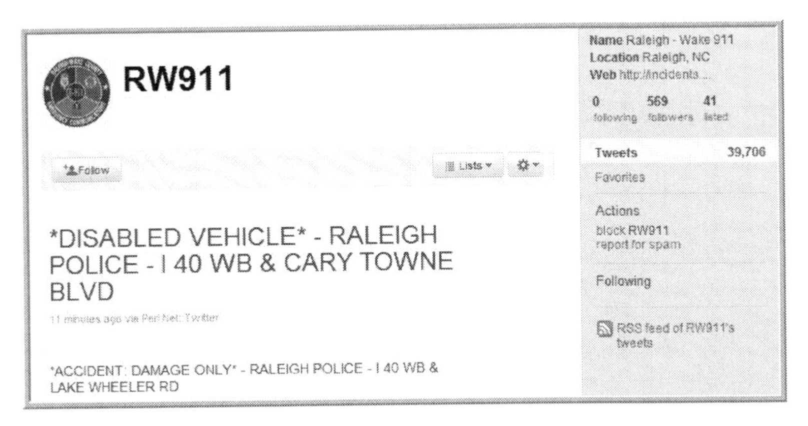

RALEIGH-WAKE 911 TWITTER ACCOUNT

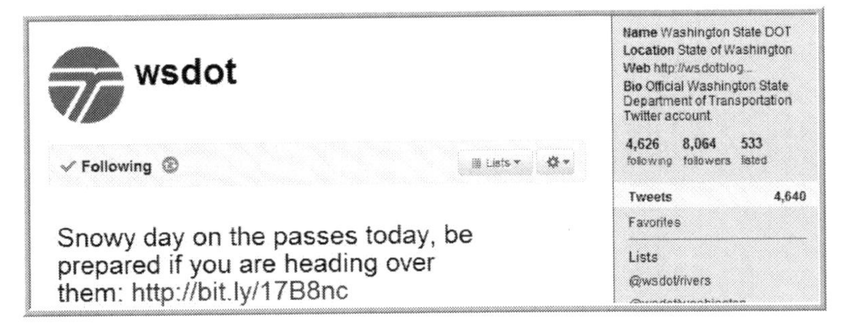

WASHINGTON STATE DEPARTMENT OF TRANSPORTATION TWITTER ACCOUNT

Washington State DOT has found that during critical times, when mass traffic to the website has overwhelmed their servers, Twitter has saved the day. It took one summer outage and an astute web guy to shift to posting urgent updates on Twitter. In a single day, their following exploded because there was a vacuum for travel information, and Twitter was the only resource available to WSDOT. That single experience clearly demonstrated to their office how useful those 140 characters were for disseminating information quickly.

Twitter and government tweeting is still in its infancy. Many are just posting and not creating dialogue. They use Twitter as a RSS feed or "push mechanism". It is difficult for many of the government tweeters to increase their following; however, some are finding some traction by appealing to specific targeted audiences. The U.S. E.P.A. branded their Twitter account under the name www.Twitter.com/@greenversations and paired it with a blog on the same topics. As a result, they have seen their following grow to 8000+ rapidly:

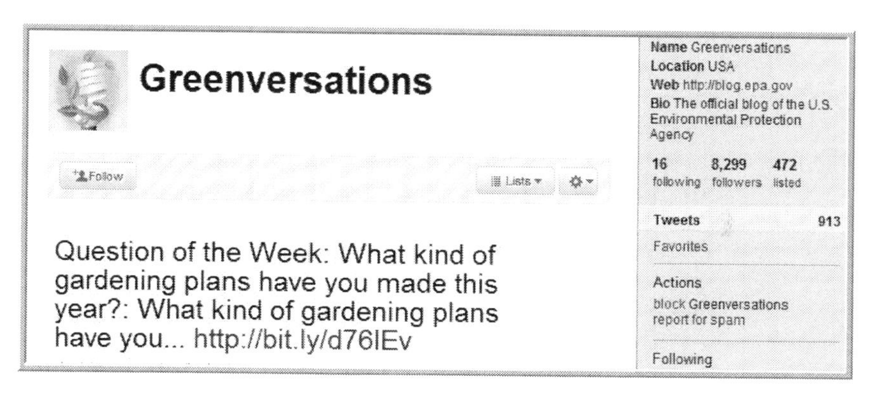

EPA'S GREEN CONVERSATIONS ON TWITTER

Case Example: *South Carolina Department of Agriculture wanted to raise awareness of state grown products and to encourage consumers to buy local. Working with Chernoff Newman, a national PR Agency, they ventured into the world of social media and created the Twitter account www.Twitter.com/certified_SC. To raise awareness of South Carolina products and to 'kick off' their initial* *campaign, giant 'local veggies' protested on the steps of the state legislature. They 'marched' to help local farmers and to get legislative dollars to fund the certified SC grown label.*

According to David Campbell, President of Chernoff-Newman, company employees tweeted the 'protest' to get people to show up and support the buy local efforts. A spontaneous 'Tweetup' at the site was promoted with T-shirt giveaways. Reporters followed the tweets and began to cover the event.

Now @certified_SC is a recognized and sought after Twitter account to brand and promote South Carolina products:

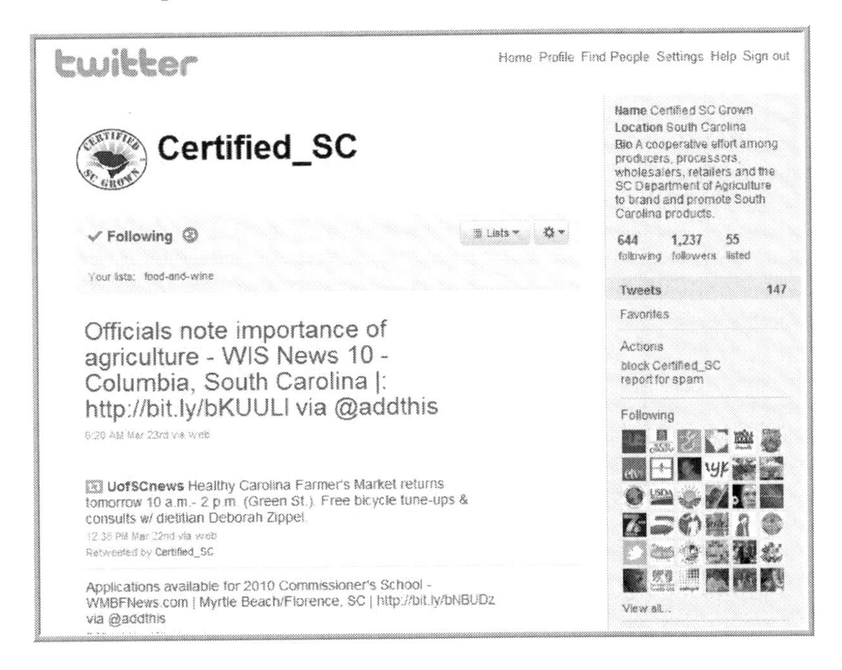

CERTIFIED SOUTH CAROLINA GROWN TWITTER ACCOUNT

With Twitter, government agencies and NPO's have a great opportunity to meet the needs of their followers, as long as they remember not to use it just for dumping automated feeds. Get in there and interact with your users, Question and Answer sessions are huge when it comes to Twitter becoming a point of customer service. When you respond directly to a follower's question, you take away the faceless entity and replace it with the personal touch. Be conversational, retweet content that is helpful to your audience, and encourage community interaction.

Chapter 15: Conclusion

Twitter is a powerful social media marketing tool for any business or organization. There is no single right or wrong way to use the tool; it all depends on your business model and the limits of your imagination.

There is a fundamental shift in how people communicate. The impact that is having on the world of business and its practices and processes is tremendous. It is critical in so many businesses that they rapidly employ strategies and techniques that allow the employees and customers to act as brand ambassadors in order to build rapport but also to increase profits and reputation.

Our world is increasingly social and new rules of engagement are mixing with old rules of business as a result of the technology that is making the global market place within anyone's reach. Social media is a dynamic part of that market now connected by the internet and mobile devices.

People are now sharing their experiences, content, and reactions at a rate of speed that makes even the best business strategist cringe. Business owners can no longer ignore the impact social media can have on their reputation, sales, and marketing efforts.

A simple tweet can have a transformative effect on a business. Businesses are learning from the disasters of Toyota, Nestle, and Maytag who failed to listen to what was happening around their brand on social media sites. Businesses that "get" social media will be able to compete successfully in the new business environment.

If a business is flexible, listens to others outside their business circle, and just follow the simple rules of any social setting they will have the opportunity to capitalize on the new markets created. Gaining insight from those who are either currently using your products and services or who are using those of your competitors can be invaluable to a business. Twitter is one piece of the new media that is giving customers and clients an outlet for sharing and communicating about products and services they use or want.

Whether listening to sentiment, mining for leads, or finding information for setting benchmarks, Twitter is a powerful free social media resource when used correctly. The power of the tool; however, is only as great as the business behind it. Engage, ask, listen, respond, and show you care. These are the social graces that are so often missing or misunderstood by businesses that implement social media in their marketing and PR efforts.

Florists, authors, tire stores, restaurants, and even local newscasters have Twitter accounts and they aren't afraid to ask you to follow them. Twitter is a great way to raise brand awareness, share and explore ideas, as well as to help get potential customers through the door or to your website.

The micro-blogging revolution is becoming firmly entrenched in the business and professional world. It is no longer just "bursts of inconsequential information." It is a uniquely quick and cost effective way to conduct two-way communications with millions of potential customers.

The seamless connection of people and businesses on the social web and the power of the new emerging mobile web technology are increasing the importance of social business skills. Businesses that combine the power of the social web with more traditional customer engagement techniques will be far more successful as the next generation of consumers matures and seeks products, services and solutions in the market place. Business must be adept at changing to meet the new styles and methods of consumer engagement in the market place.

The individual now can have a voice, a platform, and a way to hook into an automatic network of like-minded people. Social media has empowered them to speak up and demand accountability from business and government. They can raise the public's level of awareness of the important issues that impact them. Businesses must listen, engage, and connect to individuals out on the social web to thrive in the market. Nurture the individual connections and communities will begin to emerge around any organization. The same is true on the social web where connections count.

Not only have the business to business and business to customer communication channels changed, so too has the language in the market place. Words like 'transparency' and 'accountability' have taken on new meaning.

Traditional business models, marketing methods, and relationship skills have morphed and changed. The impact of this change has been felt beyond business and extends now into politics and philanthropy. The social web has changed society irrevocably. The world is suddenly smaller and information is more accessible in an instant. The level of connectivity of the world has changed and influenced our social rules in a way that now transcends cultural, business, political and philanthropic rules and practices.

Disclaimer:

This book is as accurate as I have been able to make it. I make no assurance any technique or suggestion described in this book will have any impact on your business what so ever. In fact, no one can guarantee social media efforts will have any impact on business success or failure. While the techniques described in this book have been used with success by many business owners there is no guarantee you will have the same results.

Shannon Evans is contributing author and editor of *Your Ultimate Sales Force* and the popular *Get Found Now – Search Secrets Exposed* series as well as multiple non-fiction books. Her books teach entrepreneurs that they must publish or perish in the Internet age where businesses must deliver a consistent and unified message. This is especially critical in this challenging environment of email, Internet, and mobile phones. Leveraging the market today requires new methods for attracting new clients. Shannon is recognized in the Puget Sound as an expert in how to make your business have a web presence rather than just a web page. Her conversational marketing techniques and practices outlined by Small Business Marketing Toolkits will see your small business presence on the web increase.

Shannon's workshops and discussion groups are much admired by local and national professional networking groups. Whether coaching entrepreneurs on the ins and outs of writing a white paper or in how to create a website that sells, her classes are all well attended and often standing room only. Her frank, down to earth approach to Internet optimization demystifies the terms SEO and SEM for the layperson and leads the participants to a hand's on session that makes them go from being one of a million to one in a million on the web.

Shannon has a wide and varied background in both the practical and the pragmatic aspects of the business world. As Co-founder of Small Business Marketing Toolkits she loves nothing better than teaching local businesses how to think globally but to be searched locally. When she is not writing or teaching she can be found coaching boys' lacrosse, biking, fishing or clamming somewhere in the Seattle metro area.

You can find Shannon:

Twitter: www.twitter.com/shannonevans

LinkedIn: www.linkedin.com/in/pshannonevans

Email: shannon@practicallocalsearch.com

Photos complements of Sue Larkin Photography

Made in the USA
Charleston, SC
30 July 2011